HOW TO GET
GREAT
RESULTS

USING THE RELATIONAL
LEADERSHIP MODEL

Robert Epperly

ISBN 978-1-63630-000-9 (Paperback)
ISBN 978-1-63630-001-6 (Digital)

Covenant Books, Inc.
11661 Hwy 707
Murrells Inlet, SC 29576
www.covenantbooks.com

CONTENTS

ACKNOWLEDGMENTS

I would like to thank God for giving me the ability to do something I never thought possible.

I would like to thank my wife and best friend, Mary, for her unending support of this project.

Taylar, your mom and I are so proud of the young lady you have become. And thank you for loving the Sooners as much as I do. Boomer!

Grandma and Papa, I wish you could be here for this. We miss you.

PART 1

Recognizing There Is a Problem

CHAPTER 1

The Beginning

The year is 2014, and RMT Technologies is still an industry leader, though they're no longer number one in many of the markets, as they had experienced over the past decade. The company has been family-owned and

> Taylar Wilson Smith assumed the role of CEO from her father.

operated for the past fifty years while being led by the patriarch and founder the entire time. During this time, there have been many ups and downs, more downs recently than ups, and now the board of directors are beginning to talk about a potential change needed at the top. The speculation from the board has been that maybe it's time they bring someone in with a fresh perspective to push the company outside their comfort zone so they can make real progress.

Taylar Wilson Smith assumed the role of CEO from her father, John, a little more than a year ago. She never dreamed it would be this tough at the top because her dad made it look so easy. Taylar is the older of the two children and was being groomed for the CEO position since she was in her teens. She's always been Daddy's little girl, but she's worked hard every day to get to where she is. She never wanted to have people think she was just given the position because of her last name. She wanted to earn it.

Both Taylar and Jack, her brother, attended the finest universities in America in preparation of eventually leading the company. Taylar learned at an early age to manage her life by lots of preparation, using task lists, and then taking time to evaluate her performance by the results she achieved. Jack learned to manage his life by how many friends he had and the parties he attended—quite different from Taylar's plan.

> Ensuring all roads lead to results.

Most of the executive staff at RMT Technologies began modeling Taylar's daily routine not long after she assumed the role of CEO—partly because they looked up to her and admired her work ethic and partly because they felt it was the new company protocol. Even those who found it difficult to live by task lists learned to use their calendars while ensuring all roads lead to results.

In many people's estimation, her team's performance to date hasn't been stellar. At best, it's been inconsistent. It's not because they haven't been creative during the tough economic times because in many ways they have been extremely innovative. They kept the company very liquid during the 2008–10 economic downturn—a time when many companies didn't survive, including several of their competitors, which is another reason why many people believe the company should be even more productive after than they are now. It's almost been a Jekyll-and-Hyde type of performance. One minute, people would say, "They're awesome." The next minute, they would say, "Wow! Who in the world made that decision?"

> She's starting to wonder if the board will ask her to step down.

This is the time of year when Taylar desperately needs Jack's help because he is really more smooth working a room than she is. Jack got the extreme extrovert genes of the family, which usually kept him up late at night partying while she was in her sorority house studying. Jack can talk to anyone, anywhere, anytime. The real reason she needs Jack is because it's that time of the year for the annual board of directors meeting, and she has been dreading it since the fiscal year-end financial statements were released. This is just another bit of ammunition to prove her performance has been less than stellar this past year. She's starting to wonder if the board will ask her to step down and put someone else in her place.

Taylar climbs the last set of stairs to the country club entrance, takes a deep breath, counts to ten, and then exhales. Before she opens the door, she whispers to herself, "What are you worried about? Your family owns the company." As Taylar walks around, talking to the group before the meeting, she overhears a few of the people talking about the need for changes at RMT. Well, not a few, more like almost everyone. It seems like nearly everyone is talking about the need for a change—that is everyone except Jack.

> She must not let herself get boxed into a corner.

Every time she walks up to a group of people, they abruptly change their conversation and start talking about something else like the latest action movie. Once it was the newest restaurant at the Hills Shopping Center that had opened or the Sugar Bowl win. She thinks to herself, *That was a really impressive victory and will be remembered for years to come. But I know they are just changing the subject when I walked up, and no one can deny it if I confront them.* Taylar knows if she plays it cool, she can make it through the evening without incident. But she must not let herself get boxed into a corner answering questions about the financial statement rollercoaster at RMT Technologies the rest of the evening. Maybe if she keeps them drinking and ordering appetizers, that'll keep them distracted. She must remain in control of the conversation throughout the evening so she can sort out the issues on Sunday evening during her weekly planning time. Her plan is to stay close to Jack so he can help deflect the direct questions about the financial statements.

CHAPTER 2

The Team

*T*aylar *Wilson Smith.* Twenty-nine years old and current CEO. She is the daughter and the eldest child of John Wilson, founder of RMT Technologies. She is married to Bill Smith who is the general manager of the most productive division of the organization. Taylar attended the finest Midwest business schools in the country and graduated with honors at both by earning over a 3.7 GPA at each. She initially struggled making the leap from high school to college but recovered nicely after her freshman year.

During her graduate work, she competed in the business school simulation challenge and won the national competition by beating out all other competitors from the finest schools across the United States. The simulation was designed to test everyone's knowledge on all facets of running a business, from recruiting to production scheduling to equipment maintenance to finance. The one negative people can say about her is that her only working experience has been at RMT Technologies, which is an area of major concern the board of directors has about Taylar's ability to lead a major corporation. She has no other real-world experience. On paper, she would make a great junior executive that was being groomed as a future CEO, but John wouldn't accept that answer. Taylar would run his company, period. John has always been a little stubborn like that.

> On paper she would make a great junior executive.

When he gets his mind set on something, it's better to just get out of his way and let him go.

Jack Wilson. COO, younger brother of Taylar, and self-professed ladies' man. Jack still enjoys the finer things in life including fast cars, nice clothes, and all the latest electronics. Jack normally has a sports car from most of the European countries and claims it's because he doesn't want to discriminate against anyone. He also used the excuse that RMT Technologies exports to the European Union, and they need to be good partners. Reality is, he just really likes Porsche, Ferrari, and BMW cars to show off to the ladies. Jack also has 4K smart TVs in every room of his house because he loves binge-watching TV series on RightNow Media @ Work and Netflix, Amazon Prime, and PureFlix during his early morning workouts.

How many people actually have forty-two-inch 4K TVs mounted behind the mirrors in their bathrooms? Jack does. His answer for this one is to keep up with Sports Center and NewsMax each morning when he gets ready for work.

> Jack didn't do as well in school barely maintaining a 3.0 GPA.

Jack didn't do as well in school, barely maintaining a 3.0 GPA, which is what his father required to continue paying for his education. Though in actuality, Jack learned as much or more than most people who received much higher GPAs than he did, he just didn't apply himself as well to get better grades. His answer was "Grades aren't everything." Another reality is, if he had completed all his assignments on time, he would have had a much higher GPA. It's just that his social schedule didn't accommodate for more study time. Jack's not stuck-up or one of those people that thinks he's better than everyone else, he just likes having money so he can buy the finer things in life.

Most people don't know it, but Jack has started his own company because what he really wants to do is create apps for everything imaginable. He thinks one day he might leave RMT Technologies and head out on his own to run a tech company. The app he's currently working on is a facial recognition app for pictures. When you take a picture of a person, it will automatically search the Internet and social media sites like Google Images, Facebook, and Instagram to locate the person's name. If you allow the app to do so, it will try to connect with the person on one of the many social media sites where they are most active. This way, if you find someone you would like to meet at the mall or at a concert but aren't great at face-to-face introductions, you can take a picture of them and try to make a connection with them on a social media site first.

> John always made it a priority to attend.

John Wilson. Founder of RMT Technologies, former CEO, and current chairman of the board of directors. John spent most of his life building his company and creating what it has become today. John worked sixty to seventy hours a week for years, pouring his blood, sweat, and tears into the company, especially those years when times were bad. But John always made it a priority to attend Taylar and Jack's activities while they were growing up. The schedule he has kept for most of his life is seven to seven daily. He would get up each day at four thirty, read his Bible and a daily devotional for twenty to thirty minutes, work out for forty-five to sixty minutes, shower, eat breakfast, and then be at his desk by seven o'clock each morning. He always lamented the fact he could get more done in the first hour and the last two hours combined than he could during the middle nine because the rest of the office staff would come in, and then there would be a myriad of interruptions. It's hard to get anything done when you are starting and stopping all day long.

John's wife, Amanda, died of congestive heart failure five years ago, and during the last year of her life, he spent as much time with her as possible. It wasn't too long after her passing that he decided it was time for a change. And the change would begin with his staff, and it was time to let them know. But who would have ever dreamed the change would include him no longer running his own company? John has decided it's time for Taylar to take over the responsibilities of CEO.

No one would be shocked by his decision. Taylar has always been John's choice for his eventual replacement because he knows she's always worked hard and genuinely cares about the employees, although some of the staff thinks she recently lost her focus over the past several months since she got married and is now considering having children. How could RMT be without a CEO for six weeks while she's out on maternity leave?

Mary Williams. CFO and confidante of Taylar. Mary and Taylar are sorority sisters and longtime friends. Mary is one of the first girls Taylar connected with at college when she pledged, which is the reason Taylar recruited her to work at RMT Technologies when the previous CFO decided to follow John's lead into retirement. Mary and Taylar meet almost every Saturday morning for breakfast to review the previous week's performance and determine if they need to tweak the plan they have in place. These meetings were especially helpful for them managing through the Great Recession of 2008 to 2010 and helped cement the confidence both Mary and Taylar now have.

John was so proud of how Taylar and Mary were able to keep the company out of financial trouble during the economic downturn and not sure if he could have done a better job. However, most of the staff believes John was the person responsible for the success, not that he ever said he was, but because he had demonstrated this type of ability over his entire career. Taylar and Mary are a great team, first and foremost, because they have relationally connected and remain con-

> Most of the staff believes John was responsible.

nected by meeting on a regular basis. They have the ability to move through problems very quickly because they have learned to communicate very candidly with one another and because they have a very high trust relationship that enables them to accomplish goals quickly. In fact, they're so good together they could be sisters, and people have asked them that very question on more than one occasion.

Karen Martinez. CIO and maybe the person with the highest IQ of the entire staff. Karen isn't the typical technology person. Many people stereotype employees in the technology trades as geeks or nerds, and most of the time, they're right. It seems many times that people with a high intelligence lack interpersonal skills, of course, unless they do something about it.

However, Karen really seems to understand how to develop relationships with people, and most of all, she's been blessed with having common sense. Sometimes the brightest people seemed to have missed that line when they were born, if you know what I mean. On the surface, Karen appears incapable of doing anything wrong. Maybe she is the model leader?

Karen has always challenged her staff to remain on or near the cutting edge of proven technology by continually learning what's new while trying to avoid being on the bleeding edge. One method she uses is to require each person in her department to attend twelve hours of self-improvement training annually. This way, each person remains aware of the latest technology on the market and has the opportunity to build a network of people for resources.

Under Karen's leadership, her staff has a three-year history of a 99.9 percent system uptime—a feat not even remotely matched by her predecessor. They seemed to have an outage every quarter. Karen was recruited by Taylar about a year after she had taken over as CEO because the former CIO had accepted a job with a petroleum company in Houston after he was offered a new opportunity. This way, she avoided having to fire her first employee, and God knows she wasn't ready.

Bill Smith. Husband of Taylar Wilson Smith and general manager of the most productive division of RMT Technologies. Bill has an extensive pedigree, and he could have worked just about anywhere, but he has chosen to follow his wife to the Midwest and work for her family. Bill is very secure in his abilities, and none of his peers thinks he has been given his job just because he is married to Taylar. He has earned everything he has gotten since he arrived. Bill is one of the best tacticians the company has on staff, and they use him often to lead meetings during their strategic planning sessions.

Jim Lopez. General manager of the third best division of RMT Technologies located in the Southwest region. Jim is a guy that has scrapped and clawed his way to the top by a tremendous amount of hard work and by furthering his education by attending night school. He is the first Lopez in his family to earn a degree of any kind, and he now has two. He received his MBA almost two years ago and hasn't stopped learning since. Jim is highly respected by his staff because of his hard work, dedication, and loyalty to his employees. Jim is the best negotiator the company has on staff, and they use him strategically when needed. During the past couple of years, he's been able to land two big contracts by using the talents he's been blessed with.

Jacob Scott. General manager of the lowest performing division located in the Southeast region. Jacob is a lifetime underachiever but hides it well. Jacob attended a great school on the west coast and received solid grades, graduating with a 3.4 GPA. On paper, Jacob should be outperforming his peers in half of the categories, but he just doesn't have the discipline or initiative to get there.

He started off incredibly energetic by creatively solving problems, developing new systems, and helping people, but the energy and creativity slowly tapered off after nearly a year or so on the job, and Taylar's not sure why. When Taylar reflects on her hiring results since assuming the role of CEO, she thinks Jacob might be the only blemish on her record. Sometimes it seems he chooses to concentrate only on the things he likes to do instead of what's in the best interest of the organization. But deep down, Taylar believes Jacob has great potential, he just doesn't put forth the effort. After Taylar hired Jacob, she developed a list of behavioral-based interview questions she now asks every potential candidate to determine if they might fit in the organization.

> When Taylar reflects on her hiring practices Jacob might be the only blemish.

David Jackson. One of the best up-and-comers in the organization and is quickly closing the gap between the number one and two performing divisions. David and Bill have initiated a friendly competition to see who will remain number one each time the quarterly financial statements are released. Thus far, Bill's division has claimed victory every quarter, but he knows he's hanging onto the lead by the smallest of margins.

David attended the finest in state college and did well, despite the fact he had to work part-time to help his parents pay for his education because they couldn't afford to send him without the help. David is extremely thankful for both his parents working long hours to help put him through college, and that's why he has decided to buy them a new house. His mother was so happy the day he took them to lunch and asked if they would mind stopping by a friend's house so he could pick up something he had left. When he pulled up in front of the house, both his parents noticed the for-sale sign in the front yard and thought it was odd he hadn't mentioned his friend was moving. Almost in unison, both of his parents realized there was a sold sign sitting on top of the sign. When they asked David what he'd left at his friend's house, he said, "The key to your new house." His mother was so overwhelmed with emotion she began to break down and couldn't talk for several minutes. His parents have never had a brand-new house before, and she loved this one already without even seeing the inside. When David and his dad got out of the car to go check out the house, his mother remained in the backseat for what seemed like half an hour, continuing to cry while trying to regain her composure. She finally managed to gather herself and looked in the mirror to check out her make-up.

His dad finally talked her into getting out of the car and going inside to take a look at their new home. When she finally stepped through the front door, the tears started flowing again as she looked at their new house. The layout was one of those open concepts where you could see from the living room to the kitchen to the dining room and all the way back into the family room.

CHAPTER 3

Planning Time

After returning home from church and lunch with her family, Taylar heads upstairs to change clothes before she begins her weekly planning in her home office. She begins her weekly routine by reviewing her personal mission statement and roles that she has in her life. Then she reads and responds to all emails she hasn't gotten to during the week. The next step is scheduling the most important meetings and activities first by adding them to her calendar and then adding the tasks she has agreed to work on when time permits. Just like every week, she always blocks out specific time on her calendar to spend with Bill, John, Jack, and Mary before committing herself to the other meetings she has been invited to. After an hour and a half, she has responded to all the requests and begins reflecting on what has happened during the past couple of weeks. Some of the questions she asks herself are "Why is RMT Technologies no more profitable today than it was four years ago?" "Am I the reason?" "Have I not done something to help the team improve?" "Have I not pushed people hard enough?" "Have I not empowered the right people?"

> She always blocks out specific time to spend with Bill, Jack, John, & Mary.

Bill happens to walk by the office door, so she asks him to come and sit down for a moment. As he is sitting down, he says, "How can I help you?" Taylar gives him one of those "How did you know what

I was going to ask?" expressions. Bill responds, "Sometimes I know you better than you know yourself."

"Okay, smarty-pants, then what question do I need to ask?"

Bill replies, "I'm not pretending to have ESP, I can just simply recognize when you need to ask a question."

After some further light banter, they finally get down to it. "Bill, I feel like RMT should be performing better than we are."

"Okay, what area concerns you the most?"

"It seems like most people are concerned with the inconsistent profit levels over the past few years. When we've brainstormed what to do in the past, the recommendations have always focused on replacing equipment, shifting products from one division to another, or talking to certain managers for not pushing personnel hard enough because they were just accepting mediocrity from their employees, but I think there is more to it than that. I don't think we've ever identified the root cause of the problem yet. We need to be more creative than we are."

Bill curiously asks, "What do you mean? When we've moved products from Jim's or Jacob's divisions to David's or mine, the performance has gone up."

"You're absolutely right it did, but what was the reason for the improved efficiency?" Taylar asked, and I was really hoping he knew the answer.

"Well, we had some newer equipment on one line that operated with greater efficiency, and with one of the other products, I remember it had to do with an idea a manager had to allow us to overcome the production problem."

> I think our problem is a leadership problem.

"Bill, what would you say if I said I think our problem is a leadership problem?"

"What kind of a leadership problem, Taylar?"

Taylar turns and faces Bill, who's still not looking at her, then says, "We've had some key midlevel managers and hourly employees leave our company during the past four years, and I bet if we dig a little deeper, we can figure out why."

Bill looks up from the floor so he is staring directly at Taylar and says, "I'm not sure how this could be your fault."

Taylar exhales and begins talking a little more quietly than she had been previously. "I can't help but remember a quote I read from John Maxwell that said something like, 'Everything relies on leadership.'[1] If that's true, it is my fault, and I must do something to change it."

Taylar gets up out of the chair and walks to the other side of the desk where her filing cabinet is located. She opens the top drawer and begins looking through the files where she places the important articles she's read, along with the participant guides and workbooks she's received when listening to people speak.

Bill finally breaks the silence when he asks, "What are you looking for?"

Taylar frustratingly replies, "I attended a conference about a year or so ago where a person spoke about what the most important part of a leader's schedule was."

Bill starts guessing because he thinks it might help by rapidly saying words. "Planning, research, work ethic, responsibility, problem solving…"

Finally, Taylar interjects, "Yes, Bill, those are all important, but I don't believe that was what he was saying." As soon as those words left her mouth, there it is in the file where she had left it. She is so excited she almost yells. "Bingo! I found it. His name is Thomas Eric Miller, and he said it has to do with relational connectivity. I'm going to give him a call in the morning to see if he can help us."

PART 2

Reaching Out
for Help

CHAPTER 4

The Consultant

Thomas Eric Miller is a dedicated student, teacher, coach, and mentor of leadership. He is always reading books, listening to podcasts, and writing blogs; he never plans to stop learning. He has always said, "The

> The day I stop learning is the day I die.

day I stop learning is the day I die." If you were to ask him if he was an expert on leadership, like some people do occasionally, he would say, "Is anyone an expert?" Not that it's impossible, because it isn't, it just takes several thousands of hours of studying, hard work, practice, and reflection. If you spend a little time studying about Earl Nightingale or Malcolm Gladwell, you can figure out how it's done. It takes about ten thousand hours.

It's a never-ending process and one that Thomas has dedicated his life to. Being a lifelong learner was just the next eventual step in the process for him. He sets annual goals and shares them with the people in his inner circle so they can help hold him accountable throughout the year. One of his favorite activities is reading new leadership books released by his favorite authors and then sharing them with the people in his inner circle and his mentors. This is just another one of the techniques he uses to develop relationships, drive engagement, and reduce turnover to help others continually learn new principles and techniques.

Thomas is a humble and down-to-earth kind of guy that comes from rural America. You know, the part of the country that's considered one of the flyover states. You know the area, the ones that aren't really considered vacation destinations but are still an important part of the United States. He's the youngest of three children and has a diverse background. He began by learning electrical and electronics construction during high school, which is why he studied electrical engineering technology in junior college. During his fourth semester at junior college, an event took place several thousand miles away on a small piece of desert in the Middle East known as Desert Shield by the United States Military and the media. It's now become known as Gulf War I. The event ran nonstop on several media outlets when it appeared war with Iraq was imminent. Since Thomas comes from a family that has served in the military during times of war, he knew it was his time to enlist, so he talked to the United States Army.

His original enlistment, Military Occupational Specialty or MOS, was military intelligence. However, in February 1991, Desert Shield turned into Desert Storm when the one-hundred-hour ground war began, and that's when his MOS was abruptly shifted to his secondary choice of twenty four tango (24T), Patriot Missile Operator, and system mechanic. Things just seem to have a way of working themselves out for the best, and he's always attributed it to God. If it weren't for the change in his MOS, he wouldn't have met his wife, the person who has become his true confidant and anchor of his life—his best friend for the last twenty-four years. They are the true meaning of opposites attract, which means there's hope for all men everywhere. So, men, don't give up, keeping looking. What was even more ironic is that both he and his wife were in the military, served in the same unit, and both from the great state of Oklahoma. Every year on their anniversary, Thomas calls it getting his contract renewed for another year.

During his enlistment, he and his wife gave birth to their only child, a daughter, a truly perfect example of human creation. *But don't let that go to your head because no one is perfect.* The military

> Things just have a way of working themselves out.

26

unit they were assigned to in 1995 was set for another deployment in the Middle East, so they had a big decision to make. Neither parent wanted to be separated from their daughter or each other, so they decided not to reenlist and head back home to Oklahoma.

It wasn't too long after the family moved back home that Thomas found a job just a short drive away. He decided to finish his undergraduate work, and then he immediately went on to receive his MBA from Southern Nazarene University, all the while watching his only daughter grow up and turn into a great young lady and move out to attend college at one of the finest universities in the country—the University of Oklahoma. There's only one.

CHAPTER 5

The Phone Call

First thing Monday morning, Taylar calls the number on the pamphlet she received at the leadership conference. The person who answered the phone informed her Thomas was out at a speaking engagement talking with senior and midlevel leaders on the east coast and would be gone for the week. But not to worry because she would make sure he received the message, and he was really good at responding to his messages. "Though it might be after five o'clock before he can call, trust me, he will."

Taylar responds to the person on the other end of the phone, "I really need to talk to him so it doesn't matter what time it is, day or night. I just need to talk with him."

> I really need to talk to him so it doesn't matter what time it is.

Thomas receives a message on his smart phone during his first break that reads: "Please call Taylar Wilson Smith. She attended one of your workshops a couple of years ago and is desperate for help, right now. She said you could call anytime at the number below."

Thomas responds with one of his typical replies, "Thank you for keeping me informed because I couldn't make this job work without your help." The words are almost never the same, but they always convey a similar message: you are part of my inner circle and I rely on you to fill a very important role in my life and you are important to me.

Thomas finishes sending the message and walks back into the room to begin the next session. He begins. "Let's review what we just covered in the previous session. Shawn, what were your takeaways?"

CHAPTER 6

Help at Last

When Taylar finally receives the call around five thirty, she is sitting at her desk at RMT Technologies, trying to complete the last item on her task list for the day. When she answers the phone, she sounds almost beaten down. "RMT Technologies, this is Taylar."

In the receiver, she hears an upbeat voice with lots of energy. "Taylar, this is Thomas. I received a message earlier this morning that you would like for me to call. How can I help you?"

Taylar exhales like a person who's been surrounded by the enemy for some time but now sees the cavalry riding in from a distance to help save her. "I need help. Where should I begin?"

> Taylar exhales like a person whose been surrounded by the enemy.

Thomas has a particular routine he keeps when talking with new people he's attempting to help, and that is "Let's start at the beginning and see where that takes us."

Taylar questioned what he meant by "from the beginning." "How far back do you really want me to go?"

"Can we start where you grew up and attended high school?" Thomas asks her.

"Oh! You mean that far back. I'm the eldest of two kids. My brother's name is John Wilson, but he goes by Jack because he thinks it makes him sound a little bit like JFK. Not that he's quite as charismatic of a leader as JFK or has saved anyone from a boating accident, but he's a good guy at heart. We attended the same public school because our parents wanted us to learn about hard work and what it means to succeed by our own efforts. Our parents attended every school play, all of our sporting events, and just about everything else we did growing up. And now that I'm leading my dad's company, I'm not sure how he did it." Her words seem to trail off like she is now somewhere in her past.

Thomas breaks the silence when he says, "Taylar, I think I have a really good handle on your foundation, so let's move on to where you attended college."

Without missing a beat, she begins again. "I went to college in the Midwest and earned a bachelor's degree in manufacturing engineering several years ago. And that's when I started working full time at RMT Technologies in the engineering department. A couple of years later, I went back to college and received an MBA. It was a great decision, and I'm really glad I did because I learned more about running a business and organizational development during that process than any other time in my career. Plus, it's really helped me develop a different perspective in my career about leading people and what they need, but don't get me wrong, I still need help getting through this because I don't have all the answers."

> Taylar pauses for a moment to gain her composure.

Taylar pauses for a moment to gain her composure because it's still painful to talk about her mom. She's not sure when, or if, she'll ever be comfortable talking about her death to other people. She still misses her every day. All those girl talks they used to have are now gone. "This brings us to the point in my career where my mom lost her battle with congestive heart failure, and that's when my dad decided it was time to step down as CEO. When he did, he appointed me as his replacement. So now you can see I've been with RMT Technologies my whole adult life. I've never worked anywhere else, and frankly, I really don't want to."

Thomas knows she could use a minute before continuing their conversation, so he takes the opportunity to provide some feedback at this point. "Taylar, it sounds like from your story you are a dedicated leader, hard worker, love your family, but it sounds like you're feeling concerned your team hasn't developed into the type of team you had hoped they would ultimately become."

Wiping the tears from her eyes and cheeks, Taylar quickly responds in the strongest voice she can muster. "You've got that right. Leadership really sucks sometimes. It's tougher than anyone ever said it would be. You hear these amazing success stories about how people led their teams through extraordinary times, and sometimes they turn those stories into movies. Did you see *Remember the Titans*? Do you think they would have ever made that movie if Herman Boone had failed to successfully integrate his team?" Taylar realizes this is more of a rhetorical question and one that doesn't necessarily need to be answered but does anyway. "I'm guessing probably not. How many people would want to go spend two hours watching a movie about a complete team failure? I mean, if you want to see something like that, go watch *The Break-Up,* and I like Vince Vaughn and Jennifer Aniston, but it was tough to make it through the entire movie. But I'm sure this is another question that doesn't need to be answered."

> It only happens by deliberate growth and always begins with self.

Thomas is actively listening to carefully analyze what Taylar's saying. He wants to be sure he has heard what she's saying and understands her concerns before he responds. It's one thing to listen to respond and another to listen to understand. This is a habit he learned a few years ago through many hours of practice. To him, it was actually more like trial and error because it didn't always go so well. He's learned, if you never attempt to get better, it'll never happen. It only happens by deliberate growth and always begins with self.

When Thomas is confident Taylar has finished, he responds, "Let's go back to your earlier question. Do you have any idea why your team hasn't developed the way you'd hoped?"

There's a short pause on the other side of the line while Taylar is searching for an answer. "Not completely, but I'm guessing I'm a big part of the problem."

Thomas quickly responds, "Sometimes you don't know what you don't know, but recognizing you might be the problem is the first step. This is always the hardest part for most leaders to accept, and sadly, some never do. It could be due to their arrogance or reluctance to change that they never see their teams develop into high-performing teams capable of accomplishing almost anything. But your answer was right, you are part of the problem. My friend and mentor has taught me that everything rises and falls on leadership.[2] Leaders are responsible for every aspect of their team's development and performance."

Taylar exhales because she knows he's right and because she's a little more at ease finally admitting the problem to someone else. Taylar interrupts Thomas before he can move on, "That's the John Maxwell quote. I told my husband I thought it was 'Everything relies on leadership.'"

Thomas nods his head in agreement and answers, "Well, I believe that's really the essence of what John was saying. He just said it a little differently than you did. Let's plan on meeting next week. I can be in your area on Monday. Can you clear your schedule to meet with me for about three hours?"

Taylar doesn't even look at her calendar before she answers. "Yes, I can."

Thomas looks down at the calendar app on his smartphone to see what time slots he has available, but he's pretty sure he can make any time work. Thomas says, "Great! Just tell me what time works best for you, and I'll block out my time."

Taylar suggests, "How about eleven to two? We can meet at a restaurant, and I can get us a table in the back where we can work without being interrupted."

> I have something I need you to work on before our next meeting.

"That will work for me," Thomas says. "All I need for you to do is send me the address of where we will meet."

"But before we hang up, I have something I need you to work on before our next meeting. You'll need to write this down, so let me know when you're ready," Thomas tells her.

Taylar reaches for the note pad directly in front of her and then says, "I'm ready go ahead."

Thomas begins by giving her a list of questions to ask her direct reports—questions she might not have ever thought to ask on her own. For that matter, most leaders not dedicated to developing people would be hesitant to ask their direct reports these questions. Some leaders really don't want to know the answers to these questions because they might have to change what they're doing, like getting out of their comfort zone for a change, and some leaders don't want to have to deal with the whole person because it takes too much of their time dealing with personality quirks or issues in someone else's personal life. This is known as the whole person approach.

As Thomas is finishing his list of questions, Taylar is shaking her head, thinking about what people might say or how they will react when she asks them these questions. Taylar finally asks, "Where did you come up with this material?"

"It's from a lifetime of learning, practicing, and reflecting on my own personal experiences. Then going back and trying different combinations to see how people react in certain situations because it's tough to find the right answer for every situation. I once was blindsided when I lost a pretty good employee a few years ago. When I asked him why he wanted to leave, he said it was because he wasn't doing what he really wanted to do. At first I got a little upset, but then I realized the problem. It was me. I hadn't been asking the right questions.

"I can also make you one guarantee. This is a process that will never be finished. You're either proactively working on relationships with your employees or you're not. It's a little like motion. You're either moving forward or backward."

"Never!" exclaims Taylar. "When I stop doing this, I stop learning and growing as a leader, and I never want to do that. I can only give what I have. If I don't continue to get better, my team doesn't get better."

PART 3

Taking Action

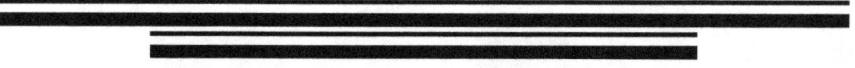

CHAPTER 7

The New Plan

Taylar sits in her chair and gathers her thoughts to finalize what she wants to send out to each of her direct reports. She needs to send the right message but not one that creates too much stress since the message will be sent by email. After several minutes of careful thinking, she is ready to begin typing the email, explaining her new plan of employee development. The organization will be a bottom-up style where the leadership will support the entire organization. Think of an inverted pyramid where the leader is on the bottom, and the entire leadership supports the whole organization. This will include key principles where developing and equipping leaders at all levels will become one of the corporation's top priorities. She believes it's imperative to get the buy-in from the senior leaders first before any new material is delivered to the frontline leaders.

> She needed to send the right message, but not one that created too much stress.

She decides to include a statement in the email about new recurring meetings or team huddles and starts to lay out the new plan:

> I will be sending each of you a meeting request so we can begin meeting one-on-one twice per month. These meetings will be scheduled for one to one and half hours each. My hope

in this process is that each of you realizes I honestly believe our company's greatest asset is our human resources. One way we can demonstrate this concept to all our employees is by the payment of our time spent with them individually. More than anything, our employees need our time and attention.

Before we meet, I have a few questions I want each of you to begin thinking about. These questions are only one of the topics we will be discussing during our biweekly meetings. Please be prepared to share your answers during our meeting as I will be sharing my answers with you. I can't wait to start this new process with each of you. I see great things in our future as we learn to develop our relationships and begin taking them to the next level.

⊕ How is our relationship, and how are we doing? We will learn to become completely open and honest about anything that might be getting in the way of our development together. This means we must have a high trust relationship. If you feel we don't have one now, I would like to learn why so we can begin working on how to develop one.

⊕ What are your core values? We will share our personal core values with each other. This way, we can establish boundaries to prevent a potential trust violation in our relationship by not violating either person's core values.

⊕ If you could do anything, what would it be? I would like you to answer this question from two perspectives. The first one is, if you never had to work for money again because you just received a large inheritance from a relative, what would you do? The second one is, if you could do anything within RMT Technologies, what would it be?

CHAPTER 8

Taylar and Jacob

Taylar decides to meet each person on their own turf, which means going to their office so they will be more at ease. She knocks on the door, walks in, and partially closes the door behind her. She suggests they sit down at the table and not across the desk from one another so the meeting is less formal. She asks Jacob, "Did you have time to work on the questions I emailed?"

Jacob responds, "Yes, I did, and I actually wrote some of the responses down on index cards to be more prepared."

"That's fantastic, Jacob. Would you mind if we go ahead and get started?"

"Not at all," Jacob says.

> Since the last time we met have I done anything that has made you mad or frustrated?

"Since the last time we met, have I done anything that has made you mad or frustrated?" Jacob looks a little surprised by this question, and he's not sure how to answer it. Taylar can read from his body language that he is hesitating, so she says, "Nothing is out of bounds here. If I've done something in the past, I need to know what it is so we can try to resolve the issue."

Jacob slowly nods his head up and down, signifying he understands her question. Taylar pauses for a moments waiting on a response. She decides to flash her trademark half-smile to put him a little more at ease and then says, "Let me state it a little differently. I'm sure there's been a time I've made you mad or frustrated, but if we never talk about it, it we'll never get resolved. Trust me, I'm not so naïve to believe that I've never done anything to make you mad or frustrated at least once in our relationship," Taylar explains.

"Well, now that you're asking it like that," Jacob very slowly and hesitantly replies. "About a year ago, I asked to take my team to Live2Lead, and I was told we didn't have the money in the budget for stuff like that. Then I learned we purchased new lightweight laptops for all the executive staff." Jacob used his fingers to make air quotes when he said *lightweight* for added effect. Like it added some importance to the words lightweight, or at least to him it did. "Don't get me wrong, Taylar, I really appreciated it, but I think the investment in our employees would have provided a bigger return than the new laptops have."

Taylar sits patiently, sipping her water, waiting for Jacob to finish his thought, then says, "I vaguely remember that. I want to make sure I get the facts right on this, so would you mind if I go back and do a little research on this topic and get back to you with an answer?"

"No, not at all," Jacob says. "That would be okay with me."

Taylar presses on to the next question hoping this hasn't just stopped any chance for progress today. "Since the last time we met, what commitment have I failed to meet?"

> Since the last time we met, what commitment have I failed to meet?

"I can't think of anything, Taylar. When you say you're going to do something, you do it, and I appreciate that quality in you." She's relieved to hear she didn't mess this one up, so she moves on to keep the meeting on track.

Taylar slides an index card in front of her with three questions written on it. She begins by reading the first one: "How do you like to be rewarded?"

"I'm not sure I understand what you're asking."

Taylar slowly takes in a deep breath and responds, "Let me explain it a little better. If you do something you would consider providing extra effort or going above and beyond, what type of reward would you like to have in return? I am asking each person on our team to provide their top three answers to this question."

Jacob says, "Okay, I've got it. I would like for my peers to recognize me for my effort. I would like to receive a personal thank-you from the executive staff about the specific performance, and finally, money is always nice."

How do you like to be given feedback?

Taylar is writing the answers and making notes on the index cards in front of her, and when she's finished, she asks the next question. "How do you like to be given feedback?"

Jacob asks another clarifying question. "I assume you mean good or bad feedback?" Taylar simply nods her head in agreement so Jacob continues. "I personally prefer face-to-face communication most of the time. You know the old saying, praise in public and criticize in private. I think that works best for me. If the feedback isn't too sensitive or isn't a subject that could be easily confused, then I don't mind email or texts. It's nearly impossible to read body language and hear tone in an email or text, unless you're typing in all caps of course. How am I doing so far, boss?" Jacob asks.

"These aren't pass-or-fail kind of questions, Jacob, but you're doing fine," Taylar answers and then moves on to the next question. "How do I earn your trust?"

"Being honest with me no matter what, and if someone has a problem with me, I want them to tell me face to face. Don't use a third party to negotiate," Jacob finished.

"I have to admit those are all very good answers, and I'm glad we've had this opportunity today to share. I only have two more questions before our time is up."

Jacob interjects, "You know, Taylar, these questions are a little different than what was in your email."

"Yes, they are, but my email did say I wanted us to work on our relationship, and I believe these questions focus on the core behaviors that our team needs to work on improving."

CHAPTER 9

Taylar and Jim

Taylar walks up to the door, and Jim is there waiting to great her. Jim extends his hand and says, "Thank you for coming to my office. I really appreciate you taking the time out of your busy schedule to come visit us. I know the employees would love to see you if there's time to walk around the building before you leave."

Taylar looks surprised by his comments but responds nicely, "I would love to talk with as many of our employees as possible before I leave."

Jim motions for them to walk to the conference table and take a seat. Jim has already prepared the room and sat a bottle of water down at each seat in preparation. Taylar takes her seat and says, "Well, okay then, let's get started."

Taylar begins her questions. "Since the last time we've met, have I done anything that has made you mad or frustrated?"

"No, you haven't," Jim quickly answers.

Taylar immediately continues to the next question. "Since the last time we met, have I failed to keep a commitment I've made?"

Jim answers again, "No, you haven't."

Taylar is surprised by how more quickly this meeting is progressing than her last one with Jacob. She thinks to herself, *Jim has either really prepared for our meeting or he doesn't want to talk about*

> **How could I serve you better?**

these questions. Taylar continues asking her questions. "How could I serve you better?"

Jim says, "I hoped a question like this would come up because this is something I've wanted to talk to you about for a while. I was a little reluctant to ask in front of the group. I could use some help on the financial metrics we use here because I'm not sure I fully understand how or why we use them. Then I would like to teach my staff what they are and why they are important to us. But before I can teach them, I need to fully understand them myself so I can be prepared to answer the questions they might have."

Taylar is taking notes while Jim is talking, and when he finishes, she suggests a solution. "Mary could spend some time with you on this topic. She loves to teach people about the financial statements and how they're calculated. This is right in her wheelhouse, and if it's okay with you, I will have her coordinate the first meeting to get the ball rolling."

> **How do I earn your trust?**

"That would be great with me, Taylar. I would love to work with Mary. I have a great deal of respect for her and her ability, and I'm sure she could help me." Jim thinks to himself, *I should have asked this question several months ago or gone straight to Mary myself. I hope I don't look helpless to my boss.*

Taylar continues with her prepared questions. "How do you like to be rewarded? How do you like to be given feedback? How do I earn your trust?"

Jim gives three fantastic answers to the last question when he says, "When what you do and what you say you do are all the same, even when there is no one watching you. When you're willing to make the right decisions even though you know it might be unpopular, but in the long run, it's what's best for the organization."

Taylar says, "Those might be the best answers I've heard so far. I think if I had given you more support, this division would be performing even better than it is. I'm sorry I have failed you, but I am willing to make a commitment right now. I will ask specific questions every time we meet to continue developing our relationship so I can start investing in you. And I am willing to listen and learn from my mistakes and to any suggestions you might have to help improve our organization."

Jim says, "I appreciate it. I couldn't ask for anything more."

"Jim, you're very important to our organization," Taylar tells him.

Next question. "What are you passionate about?"

"I didn't expect that question," Jim says. He gently rubs his goatee for a couple of seconds and says, "I would say number one is taking care of my family. After that, it is learning everything I can about running our business so I can become a better leader."

Taylar looks down at her watch and says, "Before I have to leave, I would like to say I sincerely appreciate you taking the time to think about the questions I sent, and I can tell you spent time preparing because the answers you provided are outstanding. It says a lot about your character as a leader. I would love to continue meeting with you so we can work on our relationship, and I would also like to help equip you further as a leader. Would that be all right with you?"

Jim says, "I would love it."

Taylar pushes her chair back and stands up. "Now let's go take a walk around your shop before I need to leave for the airport."

CHAPTER 10

Taylar and David

Taylar arrives at David's office, and he's nowhere to be found. She walks in and sits down at the table that has papers stacked all over it. He is clearly less organized than most of the other members of her staff, but somehow he always gets his reports turned in on time. At eight fifteen, David finally walks through the door, cursing, and throws his safety glasses down on the desk.

Taylar calmly asks, "Is there a problem?"

David responds loudly, "I don't think they could do anything right unless I was out there holding their hand."

Taylar calms herself by counting silently before responding. She knows she should not match his high emotional level at this moment because that won't help the situation. "David, could you be a little more specific? What exactly are they doing that is so terrible?"

"I tell them the plan, and then they can't execute it to save their lives. I swear, sometimes I think I need to have all of their hearing checked. They never listen to me! And they must be led by the hand from beginning to end on every project. It doesn't matter if I write the steps down one by one on a sheet of paper or a white board, they still don't get it. It almost seems like if those people have to work, they'll catch some sort of a plague. No one wants any responsibility

> They never listen to me!

around here except for me. Maybe I should just fire all of them and start over!" David exclaimed.

Taylar continues her line of questioning. "David, I can see you're clearly frustrated, but let me ask it this way. When your team is developing a new plan, how many people are involved in that process?"

David almost laughs out loud when he answers that question. "What are you talking about? It's just me. They couldn't plan their way out of a cardboard box with an opening at each end with the instructions written on the inside of the box."

Taylar is doing her best to remain calm and to not match David's level of frustration and emotion because it's tempting to just tell him to pack his stuff and hit the bricks. But at the moment, that isn't a viable option. Exhaling silently to control her breathing, Taylar starts counting again to control herself before she speaks. "Do you think that might be part of the problem?" Taylar finally responds.

"Why would that be a problem, Taylar?" David says sternly.

"Well, David, I would say it's because they're not included in developing the plan, so you never get their buy-in on any of the projects. And as long as that behavior continues, you'll continue to be disappointed and frustrated by their performance, or in your opinion, their lack of performance. Our time is almost up here, and we didn't have a chance to get to the questions I wanted to talk about. I will schedule another meeting in a couple of days so we can continue our conversation and then get to what I had planned."

Taylar looks up from her notes so she's now looking David directly in the eyes and says, "I expect the next meeting to start on time."

David draws in a deep breath and then slowly exhales while rolling his eyes because he knows he's not going to say what he really wants to. Somehow, he forces out the words calmly instead. "Yes ma'am."

CHAPTER 11

Taylar and Bill

> How can she possibly mentor her own husband?

Taylar closes her car door and starts the short walk toward the front door of the central division. She knows this potentially will be the hardest of all the one-on-ones that are scheduled with her direct reports. *How can I possibly mentor my own husband?* she thinks to herself. She's been struggling with this dilemma for the past five days and continues arriving at the same conclusion; it will never work. She puts on her best smile, pulls the large smoked glass door open, and walks in. As she makes the short walk upstairs to Bill's office, the mental debate is over, she knows what she'll do.

As she reaches Bill's office, she stops to knock on the door before entering. "Bill, would it be all right to sit at the table?"

"Sure, Taylar, not a problem."

"Bill, I've been thinking about this meeting for several days, and since we rarely talk shop at home, we haven't had a chance to talk about these meetings. I've come to the conclusion that I can't be the person to have this meeting with you. I believe it would be best for our marriage, long-term, if you met with someone else. The only question I haven't answered yet is who. I believe the best two choices are Karen or Thomas, our consultant. Do you have a preference?"

"I know Karen well and think she is a fine leader, I could easily work with her. There's no need to have the consultant meet with me.

Just because I'm the CEO's husband doesn't mean there's any need for special treatment."

"Well, it's settled. I would like to ask you three questions."

"All right, let's hear them."

"Since the last time we met, have I done anything that has made you mad or frustrated you?"

"Now that you mention it, you wouldn't wear that outfit to bed last weekend."

"Oh! My gosh, Bill, can you be serious for five minutes please?"

Bill kind of half-smiles and says, "Sure, just for you. No, you haven't done anything that has made me mad."

CHAPTER 12

The Meeting

Taylar is already seated at the table working on her notes when Thomas finally pulls into the parking lot at eight minutes until eleven. The hostess greets Thomas near the front door and walks him through the restaurant to the back corner and excuses herself. After a quick greeting, Thomas pulls out a chair and sits down. He kicks off the conversation by saying, "Clever name for a restaurant. Not sure if I would've ever thought of something as unique as this. When you first told me the restaurant name was 'A Salt and Battery,' I heard 'Assault and Battery,' so I wasn't sure what to expect. But it looks nice, and by the incredible service, I'll assume you're a regular."

"Yes, I am. Though they would have great service regardless of me being a regular or not, and good thing, because there aren't many choices in this small town."

Thomas turns his body so he can survey the entire restaurant. He thinks to himself it seems odd they're the only ones seated. He turns back toward Taylar to ask, "Are we a little early for the regular customers or did you rent the place out?"

Taylar grins, pauses briefly, and then responds, "Yes, we are a little early. Most people don't show up until around noon. I thought we would need time to work without interruption, so we should have about an hour before the regular crowd shows up."

Thomas sort of shakes his head in agreement because he likes her thinking. "All right then, are you ready to get started?" Thomas asks.

"I would love to," Taylar says.

Thomas starts by saying, "Take me through the results of the one-on-one meetings?"

Taylar organizes her notes and begins. "Here's what I've learned."

Jacob
Rewards:

- He likes to be recognized by his peers when he gives extra effort or solves a difficult problem.
- He would like for the executive staff to personally thank him when he gives extra effort or solves a difficult problem.
- He also perceives a pay raise as a reward.
- Feedback:
- He prefers face-to-face communication.
- He wants to be praised both privately and publicly.
- He will accept other methods like email or texting if the message isn't controversial.

Trust:

- Integrity
- Honesty
- Leading by example

Jacob is externally motivated, which explains his answer to the first two rewards. I also learned from Jacob that several months ago he was told he couldn't attend a leadership conference because there wasn't money in the budget, but we bought new laptops for the executive staff even though we had said we didn't have the money. I need to do a little more research on this subject and find out all the details so I can give him an answer the next time we meet, but it looks like he was right.

Jim
Rewards:

- He likes to be given the opportunity to learn new things and be creative. He said he needs to learn something new or be creative on a weekly basis to remain engaged.
- He likes to be given challenging projects to problem-solve while working in small teams.
- He likes his peers to recognize his accomplishments after he has solved a difficult problem.

Feedback:

- He likes frequent, concise feedback to make sure he doesn't drift too far left or right.
- He prefers face-to-face communication.
- He can accept constructive criticism in public as long as it is constructive and focuses on the problem. If it is about his decision-making, he wants the feedback in private.

Trust:

- He values high-trust relationships so he can be candid when talking. He believes it saves time so he can get back to working on other problems.

- He believes when a leader's actions and words are aligned, they build credibility for themselves.
- Last but very important to Jim is doing what's right even when no one is looking.

Jim might be the best person at developing people out of all our general managers. I think it might be because one of his main values is family first. I believe that carries over into his work life. He is internally motivated and doesn't require a lot of maintenance in this area.

> This was my most troubling meeting.

"David was my most troubling meeting because I realized how much of an autocratic leader he really is. He showed up fifteen minutes late and then proceeded to vent for the first five minutes or so of our conversation about how bad his employees are. When I pressed him on the subject, he started to get very defensive."

Taylar's facial expression says it all; Thomas knows she understands how poorly her meeting went. He could sense she was struggling to find an answer as to why David's division was performing so well so he took the opportunity to ask some probing questions.

Thomas began, "Taylar, do you know why I recommended you go to each of your general managers' office for this meeting?" He can see Taylar is searching for an answer.

After a long awkward pause, she finally answers, "No, I'm not sure."

"This was something I learned from studying Abraham Lincoln," Thomas continued. "He always met people on their own turf. He wanted them to be comfortable in their own setting. One of the main points was for them not to feel as if they were being called onto the carpet. This would allow them to be more willing to open up and share what they're thinking and feeling without being intimidated by being called to your office. Taylar, it would seem that it has worked so far with Jacob and Jim." Thomas paused for a moment to let that sink in before he continued to begin working through the issue with David. "Now let's see if we can figure out the root cause of David's problem. What specific characteristics have you learned about David's behavior and leadership style?"

Taylar scanned her notes from her conversation with David before answering the question. "Let's see, he started off being fifteen minutes late to our meeting, which meant he didn't respect my time, and if he doesn't respect my time, he won't respect his employees. He leads his team using an authoritarian style of leadership, demonstrated by his need for the individual control of all projects and further characterized by the micromanaging of his team. He's very dominating in his behavior. I bet if I were to ask his team members, they would say they get to provide very little input on projects, most decisions are based solely on his ideas, and he doesn't accept any advice from any of them. I would also bet that his inner circle at work includes just one person—himself. I believe he is a control freak and narcissist."

Taylar shifted in her seat a little when she began talking about Bill and his responses. "When he finally got serious, he had some good answers to the questions as well. I'll say it was a little uncomfortable doing this with my husband, so I used one of your suggestions. I gave him two choices about potential mentors, and he chose Karen."

Bill
Rewards:

- He likes to be recognized by his peers when he has given extra effort.
- He likes to be able to travel to Europe and look at new equipment and technology.
- He would like more pay raises because he knows I make more money than he does. But that's not going to change any time soon.

Feedback:

- He only wants face-to-face communication. No emails or text messages.
- He prefers not to be praised in front of the entire corporation.
- He likes to have 360-degree assessments so employees and peers can point out areas of improvement and blind spots.

Trust:

- Keep your word
- When your words and actions are aligned
- Don't allow others to gossip to you

Thomas pauses for moment to make sure Taylar is finished giving the update on four of her direct reports before he begins his response. "Is that all?" Thomas asks her.

Taylar quickly scans her notes once more then says, "Yes, I believe it is."

Thomas begins, "I'm sure you realize this, but at some point, you will have to meet with all your direct reports and go through this same process with them. But starting with these four individuals makes perfect sense to me, and I would've probably made the same decision if I were in your position. If you don't mind, I would like to provide some specific feedback on each person then move on to a model I have developed for generating great results. I would like to begin by sharing something with you about me before I provide any feedback about what you're doing. This way, we can continue working on developing trust in our relationship, which is going to be very vital if I'm going to be able to help you. I don't want you to think I'm just here to listen to your problems, provide some suggestions, and then send you on your way. We must develop a trusting relationship as well or this might sound a little like smoke and mirrors or come across condescending."

CHAPTER 13

Feedback

"When I begin a new relationship with someone, I start by giving smart trust to the other person at the onset. So together, we're able to move through problems and certain relational situations with more speed. Let me make sure I'm clear on this. I lead with trust, but I'm not gullible. I believe it's a leader's job to extend trust first and then inspire others to trust. This is the opposite way many leaders I've worked with in the past go about developing relationships. Many of them make you earn their trust very slowly over time. Choosing that path in relationship-building requires a lot of time to develop relationships. Employees are required to produce results quickly or they're deemed untrustworthy, unreliable, lazy, incapable, or simply below average by their managers and cut loose. I believe this all stems from a phrase made popular by President Ronald Reagan, 'Trust but verify.' I'm not saying all managers who choose to use this tactic are micromanagers because they're not. Some managers just get stuck in the trust-but-verify circle and never back off or are too slow to back off. When this happens, the managers fail to extend more trust to their employees so they can continue developing the relationship. This causes the employee to disengage and only produce limited or minimal results. During this downward spiral, their morale drops, and some of them start leaving the organization for an environment more engaging and with more freedom—an environment where they are being led and not managed. anyone can be managed for a period of time, but people always produce better results when they are being led.

"My definition of this behavior is called 'low trust and too much verify.' I'm also not saying there isn't a time and place for this behavior because every leader must learn to follow up on their responsibilities or lose their job. But there must be a balance so the employee feels like they can be creative and solve problems without someone constantly looking over their shoulder. Otherwise, employees won't ever take a risk and try something new because they have little or no freedom to do so.[3] Here's another example of how micromanagers fail. They get so bent on getting results, they fail to establish anything more than superficial relationships with their employees. The only time some managers spend individually with their employees is following up on their assignments. After they receive the update on their assignments, the employee is dismissed to go back to work. Some managers never ask questions about their employees' spouse or significant other, children, hobbies, etc., so as a result, they never end up developing the whole person. So the only way to produce results is by micromanaging them. When the manager backs off, their employees go back to giving minimal effort again because they are not fully engaged. The result is a low-trust relationship. The cycle could be drawn as an alternating current sine wave, where there are peaks of high performance and valleys of minimal results. I've developed an example to help explain what I'm talking about. It goes like this.

"My relationship with an employee could be compared to a box of marbles. Marbles come in all sorts of sizes, shapes, and colors. They're cool to play with, sometimes intriguing to look at, but when they represent the relationship, a person can more clearly see the opportunities they are being given at the beginning of relationship. Most of the time, this really energizes the person, especially when they see there are fifteen or twenty marbles inside the box instead of two or three. More importantly, they are relieved to know they won't be micromanaged for a significant amount of time. They also realize they have been given the latitude to make some decisions without

> Some managers never ask questions.

having to run everything by me. We do this by teaching them the boundaries in the job—how they keep their job, how they could lose their job—and this enables this person to open up and be more creative. During this conversation, we also set boundaries in their decision-making so they clearly understand where they should be working and making decisions. By the end of our conversation, we have worked out all the boundaries so there is no gray area for them to be confused. As the relationship develops, I add marbles to the box. If they make a poor decision or drop the ball on a project, I might take marbles out of the box."

Thomas looks directly at Taylar to make sure she is still on track and doesn't have a question to this point. "Are we good to keep moving or should I stop for a moment?" Thomas questions.

"Yes, we are good to keep moving on because this is very interesting," Taylar tells him. "This is the exact opposite approach that most management classes I have attended in the past have taught."

> I believe all people were created to do good things.

Thomas grins and nods his head in agreement. He knows she has only heard the good part, and with almost every application, there is the good and the bad. Thomas begins again, "The reason I've chosen to use this method is because I believe all people were created as relational beings to do good things, be successful in their own way, learn to use their strengths and talents in ways they never have in the past, and everyone wants to be part of a winning team. I have met very few people in my lifetime that I would say did not want at least some of these things.

"When I am in relationships that are just the opposite of the one I am describing, I feel like someone has strapped a parachute to my back and forced me to walk all day doing my job with the added resistance. It causes me to disengage in my work and provide less effort. I feel I am being micromanaged, and I hate to be micromanaged. I will only work the amount of time required to get the job done and then go home and try to fill that void by another means. Most times, it means I play a lot of videos game where I can blow stuff up because when guys need to vent, they like to shoot things and blow stuff up.

"I haven't always gotten this right either. I'm not perfect and I never will be and those inside my inner circle get a kick out of giving me a hard time when I mess up. Plus, I'm sure you know there are always tradeoffs in every situation that must be considered.

> I have been taken advantage by some people in the past.

"Let me tell you about some of the times when this method hasn't worked. I have been taken advantage of by some people in the past that used our relationship for the wrong results. When I've spent time reflecting on how it might have happened, I came to this conclusion. It was when I was working with people that did not have high moral character, and they seemed to make bad character decisions. They might have been politically motivated or just cared about getting a promotion more than creating results for the team. People who are externally motivated can sometimes be perceived like this. Please hear me on this. Not all externally motivated people are bad and make bad decisions, you will have to learn how to determine which ones are which. Some of these individuals simply need to be held accountable for their actions, and some just need your time, attention, and feedback. Internally motivated individuals need your time and attention as well, but their internal wiring helps them motive themselves." Thomas stops to ask Taylar, "Are you still following me or should I back up and cover something again?"

Taylar shakes her head, signifying she's got it. "No, I'm right on track with you. Just give me a moment to process what you're saying and compare it to the feedback I've gotten from my staff," Taylar replies to him.

Thomas stands up and says, "I'll excuse myself for a moment to give you a couple of minutes to finish what you're doing." Thomas turns and walks toward the front door.

*****

59

Thomas returns to the table after a few minutes and sits back down to pick up where they left off. "Are we ready to move on?" he asks.

Taylar finishes writing her last note and says, "Yes, I believe I am."

"Good," Thomas replies. "What I would like to share with you now is called the *Relational Leader Model*. We'll take it one step at a time so it's easier to understand, and we can talk ourselves through the theory behind it." Thomas pulls out a notepad from his backpack and begins drawing. He spins the notepad around so she can read it from her point of view and says, "Here's where I'd like to begin."

Example 1

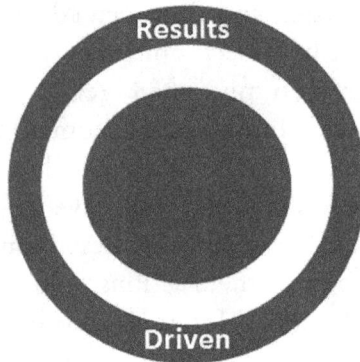

Thomas begins the explanation by asking a question. "What's one of the most important things for a leader to produce regularly?"

Taylar responds, a little unsure of the answer, "I'm guessing by the example here, it's to get results."

"Right, all leaders value results because that's what keeps the doors open. It doesn't matter if your business is for profit or non-profit, both types of organizations require results in order to stay in business. Many leaders use results as their measuring stick in relationships."

Taylar interjects, "I'm not sure what you mean by that."

Thomas waits for her to finish and then responds, "Some leaders will only increase their level of trust in a relationship with an employee based on the amount and quality of positive results an employee produces, so it becomes the only way the relationship can develop. This makes some employees feel as though they are only given freedom to try new ideas or techniques by producing positive results, and we know everyone makes mistakes. We're all human. Unfortunately during this process, employees are being micromanaged and are not given much leeway on creativity or allowed to try out their own ideas. When an employee is micromanaged for a long time, and the amount of time is slightly different with every person, they become frustrated and only give minimal effort. The leader must remain cognizant of what they're doing and for how long because it could lower the employee's morale, causing them to only give minimal effort and start looking for an exit strategy. This is just one of the ways leaders establish relationships with employees. We'll get to the other half in a little bit.

> When a person is micro-managed for a long time.

"Earlier, I said this type of leader prevents the relationship from developing into one with high trust, while other leaders, gradually over time, give more responsibility to the employee so they can determine how much the employee can handle. This is normally a better method to use to determine the maximum amount of responsibility and stress a person can handle in any given situation. Certainly, this can change over time as employees grow, develop, and learn to handle certain situations without using high emotions to get their point across to employees. It's very important to manage your emotions for your employee's sake. Now, there will be times in certain situations that do require high emotions but not every situation requires that behavior. Otherwise, people will label you as a ticking time bomb because they'll never know what will ignite the fuse and cause you to blow up.

"Most leaders use employee results to determine whether or not to give a pay raise during the annual performance review. After employees deliver results on a consistent basis over several months, the next evolutionary step in employee progression might be to promote them. Then the stress and responsibility process will begin all over again because the employee is now in a new role." Thomas decides to pause for a moment to ask a question. "Does anyone on your executive team not value results?"

Taylar quickly responds, "No, I believe we all do, otherwise we wouldn't still be in business."

"Great, then RMT Technologies is no different in this regard than any other business. Everyone values results," Thomas declared. Thomas is feeling confident she's got it and decides to push on to the next example. "I believe you've got the part of the model about how micromanagers or authoritarian-style leaders get results, so let's push on. You told me when you scheduled the meetings with your direct reports, you sent them a meeting invitation so it would be placed on both of your calendars. Inside the meeting invitation, you included the purpose of the meeting and the three questions you would ask each one of them to answer during the meeting."

Taylar is shaking her head in agreement as she follows Thomas through his next example. Thomas looks up from the notepad and can see Taylar is processing the information and knows she's still on track. He rotates the notepad around so he can add the next step in the model to the picture. After he's finished, he turns the notepad back around to Taylar to reveal her method for driving results.

Example 2

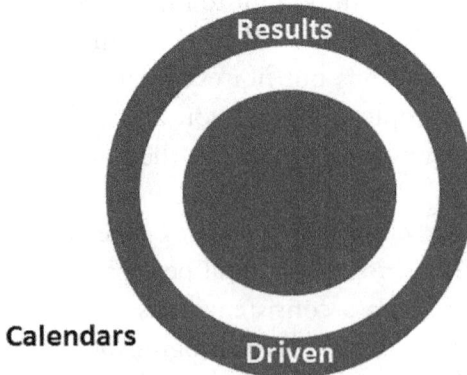

"This would lead me to believe that you used your calendar to drive results with your team on this subject. Do you agree?" Thomas asks her.

Taylar looks at the example and thinks about her own intentions and actions she has used when scheduling the meetings with her team. After a couple of seconds, she says, "Yes, I would agree, but it isn't the only method I use to get results on a regular basis."

Thomas responds to her, "Me either, I typically use two methods to gain results because I believe they are the most effective for my leadership style and character traits. Let me be clear on this before we move on. I'm not saying you should only use one of these methods because they are better than the rest. I believe these first two styles are the most commonly used and can be really effective for most people. What I am saying is a person will choose the best style for them to get the results they desire.

"Another interesting fact I've learned is that I sometimes need to use different methods when dealing with different employee personalities. Let me show you another example to explain what I mean." Thomas turns the notepad back around to add the next example to the page. When he's finished, he turns it back around so Taylar can read and think about it for a second. After a few seconds of silence, Thomas begins again. "This is the other method I believe you use to gain results with your team. Would you agree?"

Taylar looks at the second example and immediately knows this is something she uses quite often. She says, "I probably use this method more often than I use calendars to get results. When we're working on very important projects that have major milestones, we frequently use this method to gain results here at RMT."

Example 3

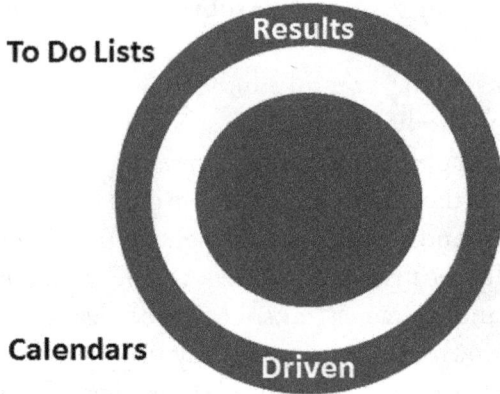

To Do Lists · Results · Calendars · Driven

Thomas decides to share a little more of the meaning behind this example. He begins this explanation by using more hand and arm movement than before. "To-do lists, task lists, Gantt charts... any of those can be very easy for visual and task-based people to understand so they immediately go out and apply them. These types of lists can quickly provide a line of sight to milestones and deadlines, which will help people focus on those things that are important much faster. I've used several different methods to keep track of these lists to become more efficient myself."

Taylar is listening intently and soaking up every word of his explanation to ensure she doesn't miss anything. Thomas is quickly searching his mind for the next example to help explain what he means. "I've used the task list feature in Outlook for this purpose. Then after it has been saved in Outlook on my PC, I can sync the list with my smart phone so I always have the list with me. I've also used smart pens that will record everything I write. When I finally return to my office, I can transfer my written words into a digital file so it can be converted into a Word document. Though eventually, I opted to use an iPad where I can type all of my tasks, meeting notes, or whatever else I want into one of the many apps. Then all of those meeting notes can be easily converted into a Word document or kept in OneNote, saved to my PC, and then emailed out when necessary. Now that Microsoft and Apple have reached some sort of agreement to have Office apps available, it will save me a couple of steps in my process. Plus I type faster than I write, which makes it better for me. But some people still like to have pencil and paper to keep track of notes and lists, and that's fine too. What's important is figuring out a system that works best for you."

> What's important, is figuring out a system that works best for you.

Thomas looks down at his watch and says, "Time is almost up if you're still planning on eating and finishing the meeting by one."

Taylar begins shuffling her papers and scribbling more thoughts so she will not lose them before she speaks. After she has written her final note, she looks up and says, "I now have a lot to work on, so stopping here would be good."

> He must continue pushing her out of her comfort zone.

Thomas knows there's a lot going on in her head right now because he's had this conversation with many people during the past few years, and he knows it can be a lot to absorb at one time. But he also realizes that Taylar needs to be given a challenge before they end today's session so she can continue developing. If he wants to make it happen, he must continue pushing her out of her comfort zone to make this happen.

He begins, "Taylar, when meeting with your team this month, I would recommend you learn what each of them is passionate about. Here are a couple of examples that have worked in the past for several people and are exactly what I use during the first few months of relationship building with new team members so I can learn if they are in the right job or not.

"Have you ever been asked if every person in your boat is rowing?" Thomas asks.

"No, I've never heard that before," Taylar says.

"In the sport of rowing, each person has a specific job. At the front of the boat is the coxswain. Yes, it's an unusual name, but they are the leader. They motivate and encourage the rowers, they steer the boat, make tactical decisions, and let the rowers know how well they're doing. The next pair of rowers are the stern pair. These are the most energetic competitive pair, but they also provide timely feedback to the coxswain. Many people on your team will follow the individuals. The next rowers are called the middle rowers. These are the most powerful rowers on the team, though they might not be the most technically skilled but are very valuable in their positions. The boat does not build speed without these four people. The final rowers are called the bow pair. These individuals are responsible for the stability and direction of the boat. It takes practice and great teamwork to be proficient at rowing. It's the leader's job to get each person in the right position so they can help produce as much momentum as possible. If one person is out of position, the boat will not win the race and maybe just go in circles. Not to mention if one of the individuals decides to make a hole in the boat instead of rowing.

"If each person is rowing in the right position in the organization, they should be capable of producing their best results. This means they are working where they are most passionate and should perform at the highest level of their potential. Many people believe less than thirty percent of workers in the world are working in an area where they can perform their best work."

Taylar interjects, "Thirty percent seems really low to me! Don't most people work in jobs they really like? If they're not, can't they just change jobs?"

Thomas says, "It isn't always that easy for some people. Some people feel like they should sacrifice their own personal happiness by working in a job they dislike in order to support their family. And some people just won't speak up because they can't stand confrontation. Many of these people end up leaving the organization to find something better. The point I've been building toward is why I continue using the word *should* and not an absolute like *will* or *always*. I believe it has to do with a theory by Frederick Herzberg, but we'll get to that the next time we meet.

> If you could do anything, what would it be?

"Here are the questions I ask to gain the knowledge about where a person's passion lies to determine if they are working in the right position. What are you the most passionate about? If you could be doing anything, what would it be? I would also recommend changing the three questions you've been asking because you have only received one good answer to them thus far. I would recommend being more direct in your line of questioning to ensure someone isn't avoiding answering one of the questions. Sometimes if you don't ask the right question, you never get the right answer. Let me show what I mean.

> What are you the most passionate about?

"Listen to the difference in how I ask you these two questions. *Since the last time we met, have I done anything that has made you mad or frustrated?* Here's the second one. *When was the last time I made you mad or frustrated?* The first question defines a specific time base in the question, which was since the last time we met. The second question asks the same information but with no time reference involved." Thomas can see by Taylar's facial expression she clearly understands the difference between the two questions.

Taylar responds, "It's like you don't know what you don't know."

"Precisely," Thomas says. "Let's move on to the next questions," he continues. "*When was the last time I failed to keep a commitment to you? How can I better serve you?* If you ask these questions humbly, it allows the other person to respond openly without feeling there will be consequences involved."

Thomas times this nicely because the food was delivered as soon as he finishes his point. As they look at each other, Taylar offers, "Bon appetit!"

CHAPTER 14

Back at the Office

> If you're not five minutes early, you're late.

Taylar knows she has a meeting scheduled at one thirty with Karen, so she quickly finishes her lunch, thanks Thomas again for meeting with her, and says she would send an email with her available times when she can meet next month after she has returned to her office.

Taylar walks down the hall to Karen's office and knocks on the door at one twenty five. This is something her dad had taught her many years ago. If you're not five minutes early, you're late. She only wished Jack would exercise this principle a little more often in his life. He's almost never early to anything. He has always applied the just in time theory to nearly everything.

After she has knocked on the door, she realizes that Karen has already prepared for the meeting by placing a set of papers on the table in front of two chairs on opposite ends of the small conference table. After they've exchanged pleasantries with each other and sat down, Taylar says, "Before we get started on what you've prepared, I would like to just talk for a few minutes. Would that would be okay?"

"Sure," Karen says.

"How's your family?" Taylar begins.

"They're doing great."

"What did you do last weekend?" Taylar continues.

"We went to the movies and watched *The Last Full Measure*. It was awesome," Karen recounts excitedly.

"Bill wants to go watch it tomorrow, so I guess I will because it's his turn to choose," Taylar tells her. "When was the last time I made you mad or frustrated?"

Karen smiles and responds, "You've changed the question."

Taylar just smiles and waits for Karen's answer.

"Taylar, we've known each other for quite some time, and I can't think of a time when I have gotten mad at you. Frustrated a little maybe at times, but never mad. Truth be told, it was probably me being a little bit selfish. For example, we would spend tons of money upgrading different areas of the company, but we never seemed to have money to upgrade our servers and networks. I would keep asking, but the answer was always no. Now that's changed in the past few months because my department has been given their share of the capital budget, and we've been upgrading all major areas that were in need."

"So are we good in this area?" Taylar asks her.

"Yes, we are," Karen says.

"When was the last time I failed to meet a commitment I had made to you?"

Karen, not so surprised, says, "You've changed this question also." Karen pauses for just a moment to think, and her eyes shift down and then back up at Taylar. She says, "Taylar, I can't think of a time when you've ever failed to meet a commitment to me."

Taylar accepts the answer and moves on to the next one. "How can I serve you better?"

Karen lets out a noticeable sigh of relief and says, "I'm glad you asked this question because I was hoping we could finally get around to talking about this. I really need more feedback than I've been getting. I'm the type of person that always wants to do a good job, but I need to know if I'm drifting a little off course. I would rather error to receiving more feedback than having to wait until I was way off course. This way, no one gets mad, and it doesn't damage our relationship.

> How can I serve you better?

"The other area where I need help is developing into a better leader. I believe I'm a good leader, but I would like to be a great leader. I know my department would be much better if I were a better leader."

Taylar replies, "Karen, I would love to help you in this area. I know you're aware that I have been working with Thomas, our consultant, to improve my skills in this area as well. He has agreed to mentor me for the next several months to help me improve so I will be able to help our entire team get better. My plan is to share everything I learn from him with our team so we can go through this entire process together. I want us all to improve, not just me.

"My first suggestion would be to meet individually with all your direct reports so you can get to know them on a more personal level. I've learned recently from Thomas if you win a person's heart, their brain can't help but follow. If we could get all of the brains in our organization working toward the same goals at the same time, we could accomplish anything. To get started, I would like for each of you to begin using the three questions I've been asking you. This way, it will push us into having tough conversations we might not otherwise have with our employees. Because sometimes, if you don't ask the right question, you don't get the answer you need to hear. Like today when I asked you, "how could I serve you better?" You were relieved I asked the question, and your employees might respond in exactly the same way as you did."

> Meet individually with all your direct reports.

"You're right because I've never asked them that question," Karen says.

"Karen, if it's all right with you, I would like to move on to a different subject so I can get an update on the status of your projects."

Karen is noticeably relieved to have finally opened up and had this conversation with Taylar. She shakes her head in agreement, reaches for the manila folder on the table, and pulls out the Gantt chart. She holds it up and then turns it toward Taylar. "You have one of these in your folder if you would like to follow along with me," Karen says.

Taylar pulls out her copy and spreads it out in front of her. "As you can see from this update, we have reached the second milestone by getting the layer three switches installed and operational at each division. All networks are one hundred percent operational, and we didn't lose any data in the process."

Taylar enthusiastically responds, "Karen, you and your team have done a fantastic job, and I appreciate all the hard work. How about taking them all out to lunch on Friday to celebrate this accomplishment? When lunch is over, surprise them by telling them they can have the rest of the day off. How does that sound?"

Karen responds with excitement, "Taylar, I think that is a fantastic idea, and I know they will really appreciate it!"

Taylar adds, "One more thing, they need to think this was your idea and not mine."

"Are you sure about this, Taylar?" Karen asks her.

"Trust me on this one," Taylar tries to reassure her. "Is it all right to move on to the next item?" Taylar asks.

> One more thing, they need to think this was your idea.

"Yes, we can," replies Karen.

"Did you get the information on the new laptop purchases from several months ago that I called about last week?" Taylar asks.

Karen nods her head and pulls out another document from the folder. "If you would pull out this piece of paper, I can provide some details for your question," Karen says.

Taylar pulls out the next document, looks it over, and then says, "Okay, take me through it."

CHAPTER 15

Taylar and Jacob

Taylar parks the rental car in the visitor parking spot at the Southeast Division of RMT Technologies and wonders why she doesn't spend more time here because the weather is gorgeous this time of year. Seventy two degrees and low humidity is a far cry from the typical weather back in the Midwest this time of year. She climbs the five steps to the front door and walks into the lobby where she is immediately greeted by two employees. After a few minutes of conversation, she walks down the hallway to Jacob's office but pauses at each office to say hello to each person and ask how they're doing. As soon as she steps to the doorway, Jacob asks her to come on in a take a seat at the table.

> How is your family doing?

Taylar begins, "How's your family doing?"

Jacob responds, "They're doing fine, thanks for asking."

"Wasn't your wife (Ashley) up for a promotion not long ago?" Taylar asks.

"Yes, she was, and she got it. She loves it so far, and she's doing a great job," Jacob says as he smiles from ear to ear.

"Have you and Ashley ever talked about having children?" Taylar asks.

"Yes, we have, but we would like to wait until she's been in this new position for at least a year," Jacob says.

"I know in the past we have talked about golf. Is that your favorite hobby?" Taylar asks.

"I really like golf and basketball. Ashley and I play golf two or three times a month at local courses here on the coast, and we really enjoy it. We're thinking about joining one of the local clubs since we play so often. Plus Ashley wants to continue exercising, even when she's pregnant, and if she's paying money for something, it will force her into using it," Jacob answers.

"Do both of you play basketball?" Taylar asks.

Jacob tries to suppress his giggling but ends up laughing out loud. Jacob's laughing is so contagious, it causes Taylar to start laughing, and she laughs to the point her eyes begin watering. Finally, when Jacob has somewhat gathered himself, he says, "You should see her trying to play basketball. It's pretty hilarious to watch. She runs with her arms flailing, and she can't run in a straight line." Jacob thinks it was best to actually get up and demonstrate her style by running around his office, and then the laughs began all over again. After a few minutes of demonstration, he sits down to catch his breath. "She'd probably kill me if she knew I was telling you this, but it's the funniest thing to watch, and that's another reason why I love her so much," Jacob says. He pauses for a moment and begins again. "She's a much better golfer than a basketball player, so I normally play with a group of guys at the local gym a couple of nights a week. She goes along with me, but she walks around the track talking to her mom on the phone almost the entire time I am playing, which is normally about an hour. I don't know how she talks on the phone that long, but she does. I normally don't have that much to say," Jacob continues.

> It's really important for couples to find activities they like to do together.

"It sounds like you guys have a great time together. It's really important for couples to find activities they like to do together. I would like to change the subject if that's okay with you."

"Absolutely," says Jacob.

"Before we get deep into our regularly scheduled agenda, I want to follow up on an issue that came up during our last meeting. There was a question about some new laptops and a leadership seminar. Here's what I found out. The support ran out on Windows 7, so we choose to keep up with technology and move forward to Windows 10 before we had issues accessing more up-to-date websites or compatibility issues with software. Plus, according to the Enterprise agreement we have, we're required to install new releases of Office, SharePoint, Exchange, Skype, and Server software annually. Karen believes in the very near future we will be required to update all operating system software on an annual basis as well. This will probably mean more frequent hardware upgrades as forced obsolescence becomes the new standard in hardware just like Software as a Service (SaaS) is the standard for software. Now, as far as the leadership seminar is concerned, I made a mistake. I was wrong and I'm sorry. I should have said yes. If I would have said yes, you might be the leadership consultant teaching our team this stuff, but instead we had to hire one from the outside," Taylar says. She is looking straight at Jacob's face

> I made a mistake. I was wrong and I'm sorry.

when she finishes her apology, waiting for a reaction or a response.

Jacob isn't sure what he is going to say because he's never had a superior own up to a mistake and apologize for anything. This is new territory to him as well. After what seems like an eternity sitting in dead silence, which is only about thirty seconds in reality, Jacob decides to say something. "Apology accepted."

"Thank you" are the first words out of Taylar's mouth. She is relieved because this could have gone several different ways, but this is the way she'd hoped it would go so they could move toward repairing the relationship and creating a better future. She continues to say, "Next time a situation like this comes up, can we agree to discuss it before it carries on for several months?" Taylar asks.

Jacob says, "I can agree to that."

Taylar smiles then slightly exhales. She's relieved to have this part of the conversation behind her. "That's great. Would it be all right to move on?" Taylar asks.

"You bet," Jacob replies.

Taylar then asks, "What's your passion?"

Jacob flashes a very curious look as though he's not sure why Taylar is asking this question.

> What's your passion?

"I've learned a great deal over the past several weeks, and this is a very important question to answer because you might not be doing the job that energizes you the most. Have you ever heard about the importance of getting every one rowing in the right position before?" Taylar asks.

"I read a book about it once," Jacob replies.

"That's really an important part of being a good leader, but it's only one part of the job. I want to teach you what I've learned, so in turn you can teach your team, and that way we all get better. Here's another way I can ask the question that might help you answer it. If you could do anything, what would it be?" Taylar asks.

"Oh! That's a tough question." Jacob begins rubbing his forehead and then moves his right hand through his hair before answering. "I would say maybe a professional golfer or a golf pro at a golf club or maybe just a beach bum." He pauses for a few seconds to let his answers sink in before continuing. "I'm just kidding about the beach bum thing," Jacob says as he laughs.

Taylar knows she's finally pushed Jacob to the point where he's going to have to get serious and tell her exactly what he's passionate about. Jacob shifts in his seat so he's sitting straight up, and he now has a serious look on his face for the first time during the conversation. He pauses just briefly and then begins talking. "I'm going to be totally serious with you. I would like for this to be the best division in the company, then the best in the United States, and then the best in the world. I'm tired of getting our butt kicked and finishing last on all the corporate financial statements every quarter. You get to the point where it just constantly beats you down, and you just accept the fact that maybe our division and our people aren't as good as the top three. You know it just wears me out thinking about it."

Taylar finally feels as though she has made progress with Jacob about why the division is underperforming. Taylar also knows she must have a nonthreatening response to keep the dialogue moving in a positive direction. She chooses to simply focus on the facts and the behaviors of what has occurred during the past several months. Taylar begins, "Jacob, I believe I have failed you during this process. You were brought into our company as a general manager and taught the technical aspect of our business, but during the process, I failed to develop you as a leader, and I want to correct that now. I would like for us to agree on how we will move forward." Taylar has learned from Thomas it is vital to clearly communicate what the new vision is and then get buy-in from each person on how the team would accomplish it. Taylar lays out the new vision in three simple sentences. She has been working on this on and off during the past couple of weeks and feels it is important to start with Jacob. When she has concluded, she waits for Jacob to ask questions. After a few clarifying questions have been asked by Jacob, he says that he understands the new plan but will need a little time to let it sink in before he can fully absorb it. He wants some time to think how he will present it to his team so they will buy into it as well.

> Have you ever developed a plan of improvement for yourself and your team?

Taylar agrees that is a good idea but wants to ask one final question before they wrap up. "Have you ever developed a plan of improvement for yourself and your team?" she asks.

"Yes, in the past, I have developed plans for both me and my team," Jacob says.

"How did it work out? Did you accomplish the goals that were identified on the plan?" Taylar follows up.

"Yes and no. Most of the time, other events would seem to happen preventing us from accomplishing our goals," Jacob responds.

"Could you give me an example of some of the events that have prevented you from accomplishing your goals in the past?" Taylar counters back.

Jacob thinks briefly for a minute and then answers her question. "Sure, sales would release their forecast for the month, and we would begin production based on the forecast. But halfway through the production run, they would change the forecast, causing us to have to shut down and change over to the new product. Now this isn't all that unusual, but the frustrating part is, they don't always give us an advanced notice of what product we are running next. So we might have the right parts in house to produce what they need or we might not. In some instances in the past, we have racked up excessive downtime, and our division is always charged the entire downtime regardless of whose fault it was, even though we were following their schedule and had the next two products ready to produce. We believe some of the downtime should be shared with the sales department. When I've talked with the sales department about this situation in the past, their answer has always been, 'We don't make the parts, we just sell them.' You know it's tough enough to keep my team motivated about making improvements in situations like this, but when our department managers won't even work together to try and resolve situations like this, it's almost impossible."

> I would like for you to develop a game plan for communicating the new vision to your team.

Taylar finishes writing some notes about Jacob's last comments then says, "I'll work on this issue with our sales department when I return to the corporate office. I would like for you to develop a game plan for communicating the new vision to your team. We can follow up with each other next week, say on Wednesday. This way, we can hold each other accountable on these topics." Taylar looks up and waits for a response from Jacob before she continues.

Jacob sits there, nodding his head slightly back and forth as to communicate his agreement, and then decides he should actually say something. "I can agree to that."

Taylar continues, "Before I leave, I would like for us to identify some goals for your leadership improvement that you can work on the remainder of this calendar year. I think we're making progress here and believe we are, so I would like for us to brainstorm some ideas with an open mind, and then we'll work on narrowing down the list. Does that work for you?" Taylar's last question is an attempt for continued buy-in from Jacob, and if he doesn't suggest attending the leadership conference he missed last year, then she will.

After just fifteen minutes of work, they have twelve ideas to choose from to begin narrowing down the list to the top three. Taylar says, "I would like for you to attend a leadership conference of your choice this year with one caveat."

> Bring back what you learn from the conference and teach it to our executive team.

Jacob perks up when he hears this and stops writing so he can listen. He focuses every ounce of his attention on what she's about to say. "I would like for you to attend a leadership conference of your choice, but I would like to challenge you to bring back what you learn from the conference and teach it to our executive team." Taylar thinks she's really starting to make progress with Jacob because this is the first time she's seen him this excited about something in a long time. All the hours spent with Thomas are paying off right here in a big way.

Just as she's about to turn back around to face the whiteboard, she has a brilliant idea—one that matches Jacob's motivational needs. She raises her left hand and shakes it slightly, indicating she has an idea. Jacob has seen this a few times in the boardroom and knows she has a good idea she's excited about because that's her telltale sign. "Two weeks after you have attended the conference of your choice, we will schedule the executive team to come here so you can teach them. This way, they can see the progress this division is making, and you can be on your turf when you teach. Make it a little more comfortable for you and a trip some place the weather is nice for a change. How does that sound?"

Jacob likes what he's hearing. He knows this could be his chance to make a great impression on the executive team, and he wants to make the most of it. Ideas start rushing into his head when he considers all of the possibilities of which conference to choose. He gets up from the conference table, walks over to his desk, and begins shuffling through the papers laying on the right side of the desk. When he finds what he's looking for, he says, "Bingo! This is the conference I would like to attend." He steps from behind the desk and walks toward Taylar and the conference table. He extends his arm and hands the conference flier to Taylar.

She rotates the flier so she can read the enormous list of speakers that will be at this conference and is surprised by the number of well-known leadership people that will be speaking at this event. As badly as she wants to suggest the entire executive team should attend this event, she refrains because she knows Jacob needs this time to be recognized by his peers. Taylar begins reading off some of the names of the guest speakers from the conference. "John Maxwell, Marcus Buckingham, Dr. Henry Cloud, Chris Hogan, Patrick Lencioni, Craig Groeschel, and Jon Gordon. This is quite an impressive list of people to get to hear speak. I'm confident this will be a great opportunity for you, and I would like for you to register for this conference as soon as possible." Taylar concludes.

Jacob is smiling from ear to ear to hear this. He's excited about the possibilities he'll have to learn and then get to choose the best material to share with the executive team.

Taylar decides it's time to move on to the next goal. "Goal number one is to attend a leadership conference and teach at least one of the concepts you learned to our executive team. What is goal number two?" Taylar asks.

> I feel like the executive staff doesn't take me serious or listen to my ideas.

Jacob suggests, "I would like to increase the influence I have with the rest of the executive staff. I feel like the executive staff doesn't take me serious or listen to my ideas since this division is always last on the financial statements. Like I'm incapable of a good idea or leading anyone because of the financial results we get."

Taylar decides to shift gears momentarily in light of Jacob's frustration to share what she's learned of the Relational Leadership Model so far. She is hoping she can hold off on teaching this until she has learned the entire model from Thomas and is confident she can answer the questions people would surely ask, but now is a perfect opportunity, and she's knows it.

> What do you think is the most important thing for all high performing leaders to achieve?

"What do you think is the most important thing for all high-performing leaders to achieve, including those on our executive staff?"

Jacob thinks for a second and answers, "To continuously improve."

Taylar knows that's a good answer as well but not quite the one she was hoping for. "I will agree that's very important because it keeps the company moving in a positive direction and creates barriers to entry for our competition. What I am looking for is being results driven. One could argue that it's similar to continuous improvement, but creating results keeps us in business. All leaders value many things, but when you boil it down to its simplest form, it's results. And results are what keep driving people to accomplish more and more every day, month, and year." Taylar begins drawing the model on the whiteboard and adds the first two methods of achieving the results. "I believe we are similar when it comes to achieving results. I believe both of us use our calendars and to-do lists to achieve those results."

"Hum. This is really cool. Did you develop this?" Jacob asks.

"No, actually I learned it from our leadership consultant I was telling you about earlier. Thomas, our consultant, is going to share the rest of it with me in about a week, and that's why this is all I have because I have not seen the entire model yet. I wanted to share the entire model with the executive staff at our next quarterly meeting, so just consider this a preview."

"Well, now I can't wait to see the rest of it," Jacob says as his face brightens.

Taylar brings the conversation back to finishing the goals list. "We have identified two of the goals so far—attend a leadership conference and teach at least one of the concepts to our executive team. The second one is increasing your influence with the executive team. What would be your third goal?" Taylar finishes.

Jacob stands up and begins walking around a bit, obviously thinking about what they have discussed so far and hoping it would point him in the right direction to locate a third goal. "I've got it!" He blurts out. "I need to improve my time management skills by blocking out time on my calendar to force myself to follow up on projects, even though I would rather be working on something else."

Taylar stands there with almost a look of amazement on her face, because in the short time she's been with Jacob, there's been a huge transformation in his thinking. She is once again reassured she's chosen the right person to lead this division but realizes many of the failures he has experienced are due to her lack of leadership. Like any good leader on a roll, they know they need to continue when the creative juices are flowing so Taylar decides to press on for more.

"We have identified the three leadership goals you would like to accomplish this year, and now we need to agree how you will accomplish these goals. The next thing we should discuss is what resources you will use and how you will share this strategy with your team," Taylar concludes. She turns toward the whiteboard and writes the categories—resources and growth.

> What resources you will use and how you will share this strategy with your team.

She turns back around to explain exactly what she means, but before she can get the words out of her mouth, Jacob starts throwing ideas. "How about on resources we include the books *The 21 Irrefutable Laws of Leadership, Training Camp, Great Leaders Grow,* and *The 360 Degree Leader*? There are some podcasts I've found on my smart phone I've started listen to when driving back and forth to work that are pretty informative.

"In the growth area, I believe I should do this same drill with each of my direct reports and then meet with them biweekly to follow up and make sure they're still on track. This way, the entire division is making an improvement together. How does that sound to you?" Jacob asks.

"I think that sounds like a great idea, and I would like to continue meeting with you on a biweekly basis as well to continue our progress." When Taylar finishes talking, she begins erasing the whiteboard and sits down opposite of Jacob. Both are relieved to have made a big first step toward improving the performance of Jacob's division. Taylar laughs and says, "You know, Bill and Jim have been on the top too long. It's time for a little more competition."

"I won't let you down. This division will be in the top two by the end of the year," Jacob declares.

They both sit there for a few seconds before Taylar breaks the silence when she says, "I need to get going because I don't want to miss my plane. If I miss this flight, the next one doesn't leave for several hours. Jacob, thank you again for being so open-minded and willing to try something new. I will continue to support you through this change, but I know you're more than capable of doing this on your own. All you needed was someone to push you in the right direction and, more importantly, to simply listen to you."

> All you needed was someone to push you in the right direction.

They both stand up, shake hands, and then Taylar gathers her stuff and walks out of the office to the parking lot. This is a big weight lifted off her shoulders, but she knows the hardest one is yet to come. How will David react? Will he be this willing to change? Will he just give up and quit? These are the very questions Taylar can't seem to answer but continues to think about over and over. But she knows she won't be able to answer them until she has that conversation with David.

CHAPTER 16

Taylar

The six-hour trip home provides ample time to continue thinking about her next meeting with David. Sitting in the airport terminal, Taylar begins thinking about what Thomas taught her about dealing with difficult people. *He said the first thing she needs to learn is what David really wants. Does he want to continue to be the general manager of his division or is there a different job he'd rather do?*

Taylar decides the first question she will ask during their meeting is to determine what David really wants to do. If he could do anything, what would it be? Taylar sits pondering that question for a moment longer. *What have I learned about his passion? What really motivates him?* David is one of the employees that have worked his way up to a general manager's position. Taylar is pretty sure he started in an entry level position about fifteen years ago. When did he get so far off track in leadership where he believes his people are incapable of doing anything? Everyone in his division can't be worthless. *I know some of those people. I've worked with them in the past. Maybe he really doesn't understand what it's like to be an hourly employee? If he's never been there, maybe he doesn't have any experiences to relate to. There's got to be something else causing this behavior. Maybe I should talk with some of his department managers before I talk with him? If I do, can I do it without him knowing? Does it matter if he knows or not?*

Something catches Taylar's attention out of the corner of her eye that distracts her. It is a couple of soldiers walking by in full uniform with camouflaged back packs and the works. Everyone in the terminal admires them as they are walking to catch their plane. Taylar just sits there thinking to herself, *That's still one of the most impressive sites to see, aside from the shock and awe in the desert. Okay, the excitement's over, back to business.*

Taylar continues thinking about her looming conversation with David while watching the people walk by her gate. Taylar says to herself, "You know, there really are all types of people in this airport ranging from young to old, professionals to vacationers, and several different ethnicities types to make it a pretty diverse place. I hope I'm not too different from the rest of them."

> It's nice to just sit and think sometimes without all the interruptions.

Taylar decides to take a break and relax for a moment. It's nice to just sit and think sometimes without all of the interruptions that normally happen back home. It helps to take time and plan out what she should do next, how she sees the conversation playing out before it takes place. *I should've started this years ago. If I would've studied leadership before this happened, I would be a much better leader right now.*

Taylar decides after she figures out what David's passion is, she'll help him to try and get whatever it is, including a different job, if that's what he wants. That will ensure he's rowing in the right position. If he decides his passion is still being a general manager at RMT, she'll ask him the four questions she's asked everyone else since he hasn't answered any of them yet. She decides to talk with a few of his department managers and hourly employees about what's been going on recently, and she doesn't care if he knows about it or not. In fact, when she meets with each of them, she will ask their permission to share their comments. If they don't want to her use their name, she'll just use the comments that were said. If they can get through all of that, and it feels right, she will move toward helping him develop some self-improvement goals. If they can't make it through those basic questions, then there's only one option that remains—a generous severance package. Better known as promoting him to a former employee.

CHAPTER 17

Emergency Phone Call

Taylar decides she needs some advice from Thomas before her meeting with David. Thomas calls at precisely ten o'clock as scheduled. After they exchange pleasantries, Taylar gets right to work asking for help about what she's learned during her most recent meetings.

"Here's what I've learned from his direct reports, and some of it's pretty troubling. I've been told David never meets with anyone on a regular basis to help develop and equip them. When he does meet with his direct reports, it's only to check up on their assignments, and as soon as that discussion is over, the meeting's over. They never talk about anything else. If a project starts going badly, he blows up out on the production floor at his department managers in front of their direct reports and anyone else that might be around. It's got to be pretty humiliating. One of the people I talked to said their intention is to wait him out. They think eventually he will either be promoted or fired. Either way they will be better off, and things can get back to normal before he arrived. I can't believe I've let it get to this point. I'm embarrassed. No wonder the turnover is so high at his division." Taylar is clearly frustrated as she's ever been with any employee. How could she not have seen this behavior before now? On the surface, it seems his division is doing quite well, but after a little digging, there could be a mass exodus

> How could she not have seen this behavior before now?

at any moment. All it's going to take is one more event to be the final straw. She hopes it's not too late to make a change.

"Here's the long and short of it. The first question is simple really. Is he worth keeping? Because if he's not, the alternative is easy." Thomas brings the conversation directly to the point where Taylar must make a decision.

Taylar doesn't answer initially but sort of talks her way into making a decision. "He started off as a really good employee, solving problems, generating good ideas to create new products, or finding new ways to produce our products cheaper or faster. The general manager at his division when he was hired couldn't stop raving about him and his performance. He could do no wrong and was a model employee. What's changed since then?" Taylar ends her dialogue with a question—one that she knows she must answer, but Thomas probably can't.

> He could do no wrong and was a model employee.

As she sits behind her desk repeatedly clicking her ink pen open and then close, it sounds like she's doing the children's nursery rhyme. Eenie, meenie, miney, moe. Catch a tiger by the toe. If he hollers, make him pay. My mom told me to pick the very best one, and that is *Y-O-U*. "I at least want to figure out what changed to send him down the path he's on. But I'll let him make the decision as to whether or not he stays. If he decides to stay, there must be major changes though. Is he worth keeping? I will let him decide. Where does that bring us?" Taylar finally answers Thomas's question and then asks one of her own.

Thomas is not surprised because half the people he works with in these situations think they can save everyone. Sometimes it works, sometimes it doesn't. Anyway, he doesn't want to waste any time getting to work on the path she's chosen. "Taylar, I would say he is a classical theoretically driven person based on what you've told me in our past conversations. Here are some of the typical characteristics of that personality type.

"They have a tendency to be micromanagers and their primary leadership style is autocratic. They do have moments when they use a different leadership style, and I believe David's secondary style is the transactional leadership style. They do not work at building relationships with their employees because it takes too much effort, and they don't want to spend the time on it. They experience high employee turnover. Their employees have low morale. They lose some of their best people and sometimes it's for a fifty cent per hour raise. They haven't figured out how to transition from a manager to a leader. They have not learned to praise in public and criticize in private.

"Taylar, can you check your email?" Thomas asks. "I just sent you an attachment that includes the next example of the Relational Leadership Model."

Taylar quickly responds, "I've got it." Taylar double-clicks on the attachment to reveal the third method leaders use to gain results. "So what you're telling me is David fits into this third category?" Taylar asks Thomas.

Example 4

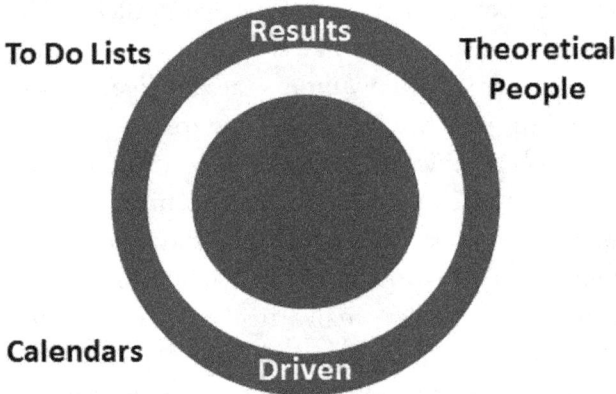

To Do Lists — Results — Theoretical People — Driven — Calendars

"Taylar, I think David fits squarely into this category. You've shared with me example after example of nearly every description I've just given you on this category. I also need you to understand that this is the hardest leadership type to be successful. This group is normally comprised of high-achieving performers who almost always struggle with developing relationships. I'm not trying to discourage you, but you've got your work cut out for you." Thomas feels Taylar is going to accept the challenge regardless of what he said, so he decides it is time to move on to the next leadership type. "Taylar, I sent you another email. But this time it has two attachments, and I only want you to open the attachment labeled number four. Let me know when you're ready." Thomas adds.

Taylar responds, "It's open. I'm ready."

"Taylar, this is the fourth and final leadership type—agendas. This is the type where some people literally use agendas to plan. They understand what the final product should look like but they don't always know every minute detail on how to get there.

Example 5

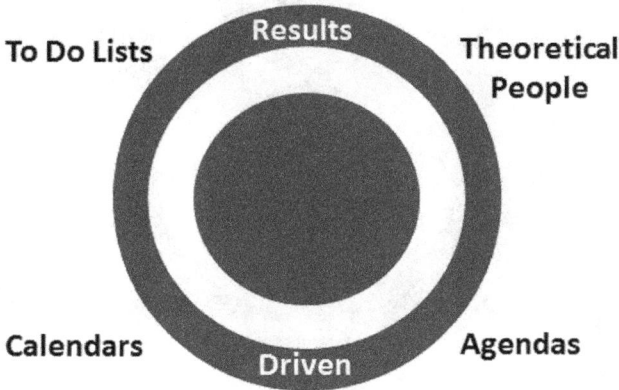

"The other half of this type is reserved for the people who are politically motivated or not very organized. These people are driven by job titles and money, and they'll tell you whatever you need to hear so they can get ahead. Or they can be good story tellers, good communicators, but not very good with details. If they are politically motivated, their opinion changes like the weather in the Midwest. One day, you have summer, and the next, you have winter. Trust me, it isn't really fun. Political people will normally follow the majority regardless of the topic or situation at hand. When you find these people in your organization, you should offer them a severance and send them down the road. The other half that fit in this category can be really good employees if they are given good boundaries. Are we good so far?" Thomas asks.

"Yes, I am," Taylar replies.

"Great, would you open the next attachment so we can move on to the next example?" Thomas asks.

"Yes, I will." Taylar closes the current graphic and then moves her mouse to double-click on the next second attachment. As it opens up on the desktop, she takes it all in, and exclaims, "Oh! This is really making sense now, Thomas. I like it."

Example 6

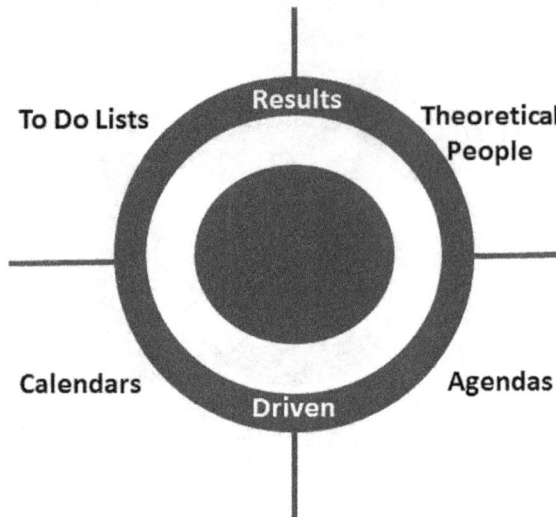

"Regardless of the method you choose to gain results, they will only take your team or organization so far. Unless you build relationships with people, you cannot make it to the next level, which is Relationally Connected Results. The only way to reach this level of the hierarchy is to dedicate time building solid relationships with your people. You must be willing to dedicate the time to develop high trust relationships with your people, and when you do, they will help you achieve results like you've never seen before.

"This process requires intentional effort and takes time. It's slow because it requires the leader to first spend time building relationships and then develop those employees with potential into leaders. For a period of time, the results will appear to drop because your team members will be learning how to interact with you and each other, and the more speed that can be developed in the relationships, the faster your team will be able to solve problems and create new processes.

"One of the biggest mistakes I see, if not the biggest, is many leaders are confused what the development process is all about. Many leaders only teach their employee's specific job-related skills, and when an employee demonstrates the ability to complete their job by delivering results, their leader assumes they will also make a good leader. This is called development, and equipping is something different. During this process, their leader has totally ignored the other areas where people need developed. For example, the soft skills like how to effectively communicate, giving feedback, how to effectively manage a confrontation with an employee, not to mention how to help people through personal issues. Without providing training in all of these areas it sets up the newly promoted employee to fail because the other areas of their life are never addressed."

> One of the biggest mistakes I see, if not the biggest, is many leaders are confused what the development process is all about.

Thomas pauses to let this sink in before he continues with the rest of the Relational Leadership Model. In the past, his clients have wanted to push back at this point because most people only measure success by results regardless how they get them. And Thomas knows it takes time to see the problem from a different perspective, especially if the person listening is part of the problem.

Taylar is leaning back in her chair with her eyes closed, sorting out all the information in her head that Thomas is sharing. She is beginning to realize she has allowed this behavior to continue since she's been at the helm. Taylar could share one bad example after the other. It's like a never-ending cycle, like the popular definition of insanity or maybe even *Ground Hog Day*. For the moment, she needs to pause to reflect on how to bring clarity on what she's inferring. Thinking to herself, she begins to mumble. "How many times have I seen examples of this over the past couple of years? For sure, several times at David's division, but there must be others as well. I know

I must be the one to change this." She continues mulling over the information as she's trying to decide the next step.

After one or two minutes of silence, Taylar begins talking again. "What I hear you saying are some leaders only teach their employees job related skills, and if the employee performs well at this level, their leader assumes they will make a good leader. The result is they get promoted and it starts all over again."

> Thomas knows she has reached the second stage of competence.

"Yes, that's exactly what I'm saying. The cycle ends up being repeated over and over until someone realizes it and decides to make a change." Thomas concludes.

Taylar exclaims, "Well, that sucks! I'm positive we're guilty of this."

Thomas knows she has reached the second stage of competence, and when she's ready, he'll walk with her to the next stage, but for now she needs to be reassured to continue. "Now that you know, you can make a change. It's not that you made a mistake because everyone does, it's how you respond that sets you apart from others," Thomas encourages.

"My daddy always taught me failure's not an option. I need help figuring out how to fix this so RMT can continue moving forward. So let's go." Taylar has always been good about not letting the little things get her down. She's been able to learn from her mistakes in the past, which has enabled her to continue to improve year after year.

Thomas takes her cue and begins where he left off. "It's not a secret that an employee's productivity is determined by their relationship with their immediate supervisor. If their immediate supervisor will motivate, teach, and inspire them, give them recognition, and reward positive performance, they will give extra back in return. Listen closely to this one. In fact, you might want to write this down. First, I want to define a new term I'm going to use. *High achieving performers* are those who've made a living producing results by completing the assignments they're given, solving problems, or generating new ideas. It doesn't mean they are or will be good leaders. Because at this point in their career, they really haven't done anything to prove they can or cannot lead people. You have to find out if they can. These individuals might simply be very good individual contributors, but terrible leaders. Make sense?" Thomas asks.

"Yes, it does," Taylar responds.

> It requires them to develop the entire person, not just part of them.

"All right, here we go. One of the main reasons high-achieving performers do not like to build relationships with people is because it's messy. It requires them to develop the entire person, not just part of them, which takes a lot of their time—which is normally something they do not want to give up. To be successful, they have to learn to help their employees through all of their problems, including those at home, personality quirks, and their attitudes because all of these areas affect a person's work performance. This process takes time away from being able to produce results, at least in the short run, and high-achieving performers normally don't want to dedicate the time it takes so they usually avoid it.

"In fact, many leadership programs used to only focus on knowledge and skills, the things that are cognitive based. Imparting things during training like values, culture differences, and attitudes were not included. But in recent years, there's been a shift because people are recognizing that soft skills are as important as technical skills. This is all about a company's culture and culture trumps everything else.

"Another reason this happens is leaders do not want to give away their power to others, which is paramount to making the transition to leadership from management. Managers want things to stay the same, while leaders embrace change.

"In the past, when I've been asked to consult for companies that have identified they have high-achieving performers in key positions ranging from the C-Suite all the way down to the frontline level, they were unable to determine what they needed to do with them. The reality is these companies have a leadership problem because most of the people in those positions are really managers

> Managers want to remain in control of everything, whereas, leaders want to teach and empower their people.

and not leaders. Do you remember what I said the difference was between the two?" Thomas interjects.

Taylar responds, "Yes, I do. Managers want things to remain the same, whereas, leaders want to teach and empower their people."

"That's a great way to put it, Taylar." Thomas decides to continue his explanation. "When these people are closely evaluated, I've noticed they hold on to or guard the information so others can't get access to it. This helps them feel needed. They like to be the center of attention. Some can be aggressive, condescending, and arrogant in their approach with people. Not all of them, and it's the leader's job to figure out which ones. Humility is a trait that some do not have. Simply, they are never taught how to transition into leadership because the person leading them didn't take the time, didn't recognize what was going on because they were producing results, and was ignorant to the drop in morale or just wrote it off as they didn't like change. Lastly, the person leading them wasn't a leader, and you can't give what you don't have.

"In some of these companies, the culture they promote limits their creativity and development. Every company will have a culture whether it's one they have created or not. If you want your company to be successful, you need to focus on getting the right culture. Another fact you might find hard to comprehend is there are people who believe only those with college degrees are capable of generating good ideas and being in leadership positions, which is a load of you-know-what. But on the flip side, there are still some good companies that make it a priority to develop all of their people not just those in leadership positions. These are the companies that have learned great ideas can come from anywhere in the organization. These companies will pluck out two or three potentially good ideas and work on them until they're completed, and then they'll go back to get a couple of more and start the process over again. These companies have learned when you win a person's heart, you get their brain. When you get their brain, you get ideas, and that's when real

> There are people who believe only those with college degrees are capable of generating good ideas.

progress can be made. I've dubbed this process as the three *L*s—look, listen, and learn. Look at the health of the organization regularly by getting out of the office and looking at all your people. Listen to your people. Listen to understand and not to respond. This means actively listening to them because most of the time, they'll help solve whatever problem you have. Teach everyone it's okay to make a mistake because we all do. The key is to learn from your mistakes and not to repeat them.

"I'm going to stop here and give you time to think and reflect on what we've discussed. I know this is a lot to think about, and it takes time to reach your own conclusions on some of these topics. I'll save the final piece of the model until we meet in person in a couple of weeks. Maybe you will be able to figure out the last part on your own. In the meantime, you have a meeting to prep for with David. I would recommend you spend some quality time thinking about what you want to say, what questions you'll ask, and how you think David might answer the questions. That will put you in a good position to accomplish what you'd like to learn during the meeting. The last piece of advice I have is one of the best ways to learn something new is to teach it to someone else. Start during a one-on-one to practice, and then after you have a feel for it, teach your entire executive staff."

Taylar thinks about it for a minute then says, "Good idea, I will."

Thomas finishes his thoughts. "If there's nothing else you need, I'll see you in two weeks." Thomas has accomplished exactly what he needed during their conversation, which was to answer all of Taylar's questions and give some advice. Plus he was able to stimulate some good thinking until they meet again. He'll get an update soon enough about how the meeting with David transpired, and he won't be surprised if she presents him with a new plan for her entire executive team.

Taylar knows he's right. She does have plenty to work on and think about before their next meeting, and she needs to get started soon. "Thanks again for agreeing to talk with me today, it's helped. I have stacks of notes to review, and I am going to take your advice and spend time thinking about what I'm going to say when I meet with David. I have some ideas about what he might say, so I'm going to spend some time preparing how I will respond to him. Thanks for everything, and I'll see you in a couple weeks." Taylar finishes.

"You're welcome, and good luck." Thomas ends and then hangs up the phone.

CHAPTER 18

Taking Thomas's Advice

Karen arrives at Taylar's office a few minutes early to find her drawing what appears to be a bull's eye on the whiteboard. "Taylar, if I was supposed to bring some darts or something, I missed the memo," Karen says as she laughs.

Taylar pauses to laugh with her because she hadn't really thought about how this might look to others when all of the details aren't included in the picture. "You know, I hadn't really thought about it like that before, but you're right. It does kind of look like a bull's eye.

"The reason I asked to meet with you today is so I could share the Relational Leadership Model with you. This is what Thomas, our management consultant, has been teaching me. But before I teach it to the executive team, I want some advice from you about how best to present it to them." Taylar says as she demonstrates her normal high-energy level, especially when she is teaching because this is one of the areas that really energizes her.

Karen responds simply, "Got it," considering everything she'd just heard Taylar say.

Taylar begins by explaining what she had planned. "I thought I might begin with showing everyone the completed model," Taylar says, pointing to the completed 'bull's eyes' to her left, and then turns to the diagram, or half-finished 'bull's eye,' on her right. "Then I would back up to the beginning and use some examples from our own employees to provide a better explanation of how these styles apply to RMT. I've spent time thinking about what style each person in our executive staff uses to drive results. For example, I believe you use calendars and task lists to get results. Mary and Bill both use task lists, Jim uses calendars, Jacob uses calendars and agendas, and David is a theoretical person."

Karen is thinking about one more person. Did Taylar leave him off the list for a reason? Surely not. "I think you left someone off the list, Taylar," Karen curiously commented.

Taylar looks down at her notes and begins counting off the names. Karen, Mary, Bill, Jim, Jacob—"

Karen can't let her keep going; she has to volunteer the name. She asks, calmly not trying to laugh, "How about Jack?"

Taylar sighs and rolls her eyes. "Oh my gosh! How could I have ever left Jaaack off the list?" She draws out the *a* when she says his name because that's how she typically says Jack when she's goofing around. On the other hand, his name also has a very distinct sound when she's mad at him. It comes out in a single syllable simple as Jack, though it's usually a little louder and higher pitched than normal. Both of them know this really isn't a question that needs answered, but Taylar wants to take a shot at it anyway. "To be honest, I'm not sure he uses anything other than the wind. He has a tendency of going wherever and whenever he wants, but somehow he's able to keep up with his assignments. He's always been that way." Taylar shakes her head slightly left to right to help her refocus on why the two of them are in the office. "Anyway back to business. What do you think?" Taylar asks.

Karen is still standing near the conference table, looking at the whiteboard and thinking about what to say next. She has a habit of talking herself through problems out loud to help her reach a solution. She begins, "I like it. It's easy to understand, but I think some people will challenge the whole relationship component depending on how you present it. Here's what I'm getting to. If you're recommending each general manager meet with all of their direct reports every two or three weeks for six months, then that's one thing, and I think they will go along with it. Some might be reluctant at first, but they'll do it.

"But if you're recommending each general manager meet with every manager, at every level, in their organization, then that's a completely different story because now you're talking about an additional four to five hours of one-on-ones alone each week."

Taylar sighs because she knows what level of commitment will be required if she asks every member of the executive staff to buy in to this. "I believe this is very important, and I have developed a plan that I believe will help move us to one number or two in every area we compete. But we must have every manager's buy-in if this is going to be successful. We don't get there without everyone helping the organization move the ball forward.

"I'm going to ask our executive staff to meet with all managers every two weeks for at least six months to see if we can turn this thing around. This will give each frontline and middle manager about eighteen hours of personal time with the general manager of their division or the C-Suite officer of their department, which should be a good start to developing high trust relationships. I also know before I ask anyone to do this, I must be willing to make the sacrifice first. Good news is I've already begun." Taylar starts popping the dry-erase marker lid off then back on repeatedly, which is something she does when she's thinking. After five or so repetitions, she turns and looks at Karen.

> I'm going to ask our executive staff to meet with all managers every two.

"Taylar, I'm already doing this so it isn't a big deal to me. But there could be a few people that might have an issue with this," Karen explains.

"Thanks for listening and the advice. I appreciate it," Taylar says. "I need to get going. I have a meeting in twenty minutes." Taylar lays down the marker on the tray and walks toward her desk to pick up an envelope. She says to herself, "*Here goes nothing.*"

PART 4

Confronting the Problem

CHAPTER 19

Taylar Confronts David

Taylar arrives five minutes early as usual, but this time David is already seated in his office and ready to go. Taylar knocks on the door and says, "Good morning, David." As she walks through the door, she continues her greeting. "It's good to see you. How was your weekend?"

David stands up to greet Taylar and motions for her to sit at the conference table with him. "Good morning to you, Taylar. My weekend was really good. I spent the weekend with my parents. We cooked out and then went to the home and garden show downtown. My mom loves those kinds of things. She's always finding some project for her and my dad to work on around the house. She loves them more than he does, believe me, but he loves her unconditionally so he goes along anyway."

> The last time we met didn't go so well, and frankly, I'm concerned about the health and culture of this Division.

In Taylar's brief estimation, David appears to be relaxed and in a pretty good mood, so she decides it's time to begin the meeting. "David, the last time we met didn't go so well, and frankly, I'm concerned about the health and culture of this division. I've spoken with several members of your team, and they're concerned as well. They're not really sure they want to continue working here much longer unless something changes. I thought the best place to start would be with this question. Here it goes. If you could have any job in RMT Technologies, what would it be?"

David looks as though he's been taken off guard by this question. He briefly pauses in attempt to control the anger in his response. He's thinking, *This cannot be the same questions she's been asking everyone else. Can it? Where is she going with this? She knows this division has been one of the top two performing divisions over the past two years, and if she doesn't remember, she can go back and look at all financial statements. Why would she want to mess up a good thing, especially when we're making money? She can't run this division without me.* David finally gathers himself to respond. "Taylar, I like my job. There are a few employees here I would still like to replace so I could make the division even better, but all things considered, I like my job. I wouldn't choose any other position right now. Maybe in a few years, but not now. Yes, it's frustrating at times, but what job isn't?" David's words are coming out more as a statement than a question.

Taylar is beginning to notice the more David talks, the more upset he appears to become. She is becoming acutely aware of the signs of anger in David's voice. His face is starting to turn a light reddish color, and his jaw muscles are tightening as if clamping down on something. She slowly moves her eyes from his cheeks to his forehead and notices a blood vessel that has popped up, indicating signs his pulse is starting to race. Taylar knew this would be tough, but now she knows David doesn't fully understand the gravity of the situation or how close he is to being promoted to a former employee. She decides to press on slowly. "David, if you're choosing to remain as the general manager of this division, you will have to agree to make some changes. This will include changes to your attitude, behavior, and the treatment of our employees. You'll have to agree to these terms or we have no deal."

> David doesn't fully understand the gravity of the situation, or how close he is to being asked to leave.

Taylar is sitting across from David, looking directly at him, and waiting on his response to her question. When she was preparing for this moment, she predicted he would deny he was the problem and start blaming everyone else, but she has vowed to not allow that to happen. She will remain firm in her decision to be tough. If Thomas has taught her anything, it's that change must start with self. If David is going to remain on the staff, he must be willing to change himself first before trying to change anyone else.

Taylar can feel the tension continuing to build like a deep fog in the room when David begins to speak. "Taylar, I appreciate your concern about my division and my employees, but if you'll tell me who you've spoken to, I'll take care of it. I can work this out on my own. I don't need help." David's response is clearly elevated in tone, and he appears to be angry more than anything else. Taylar recognizes David is on the verge of a meltdown, so she decides to step out of the current conversation in an attempt to make progress. Otherwise there's only one option remaining, and she has brought the document with her just in case.

Taylar shifts gears to see if she can help David calm down. "David, I have failed you because I failed to lead. In fact, I have failed the entire executive staff because I failed to lead, develop, and equip them. I have not provided training, resources, or timely feedback to help create the culture we need to keep moving our organization forward. And I didn't come here today to tell you this was all your fault. I openly accept some of the blame, but you must be willing to assume some of it as well. What I did want to talk about was how we might develop a plan together to change the culture of this division." The color is beginning to return to David's face, and he finally appears to have calmed down to a point where they can continue, so Taylar decides to move back into the conversation. "David, would you be willing to work with me in creating a plan to change the culture of this division?" Taylar calmly asks.

David clears his throat and drawls in a deep breath before he begins his response. "Taylar, I can't believe for a second you think I'm the problem here." His words have been elevated a couple of decibels since he began speaking, almost to the level of the last time he spoke. "I work anywhere from sixty to seventy hours a week to make sure all of our orders are completed on time and we meet our customer requirements. No one else in this division or probably anywhere else in our organization can say they do that."

> What I'm saying is that I don't appreciate the way our employees are being treated.

Thomas was right. He is denying all of it. She has prepared herself for this response. "David, I am not saying you don't work hard or that I don't appreciate your effort because I do. What I'm saying is that I don't appreciate the way our employees are being treated, and they're not being developed into leaders. I believe somewhere between twenty and thirty percent of your day should be spent on building relationships and developing people. We must prepare the next generation of leaders to lead, and we're not doing that. Again, I will concede I failed in developing our executive staff, and that's why you are being given a second chance. I didn't model the correct behavior for you. But I am now. I need your commitment that we will develop a plan so we can begin this journey together.

CHAPTER 20

Introducing the Model to the Team—Executive Staff Meeting One

"Here's the reason I've called this meeting. As you know, I have been meeting with a leadership consultant to help us all become better leaders so we can help move our company forward to the next level. What I've learned during this process is our company is littered with a behavior or personality type known as a *high-achieving performer*. This is a person that might have started in an hourly position and outperformed their peers, so they were promoted to an entry level leadership position. Not only is this typical for us, but we've all agreed in the past, when all things were equal, we always promote from the inside. This provides our employees with hope and the possibility of moving up in our organization instead of having to leave our company to get promoted. This *high-achieving performer* could also have been brought in from the outside and placed directly into a leadership position because we didn't have the right internal candidate to fill the position. Regardless of the path, this person might have taken along the way we failed to develop them into leaders, and as a result of our

> What I've learned during this process is, our company is littered with a behavior known as the *High Achieving Performer* .

failure, they did what they know. They micromanaged their teams, they controlled the information, never extended trust, and they didn't spend any real time getting to know each of their team members. As a result, they never developed anything more than superficial relationships, which drove morale down and turnover up. Another thing I have learned during this process is that not all good technicians turn into great leaders.

"If you were managing one of these *high-achieving performers*, you probably thought they were doing a good job because their teams produced positive short-term results. Some people only recognized there was a problem after key people on their team left the company, which in many cases is usually too late to help correct the *high-achieving performer's* behavior. When a *high-achieving performer* pushes their team to this point, it can be very difficult for them to ever be effective again—not that it can't happen, it just takes a great deal of effort, humility, and work developing solid relationships. And humility is a character trait almost every *high achieving performer* lacks.

> *High Achieving Performers* will normally only listen to their boss.

"Another fact of these *high-achieving performers* is, they will normally only listen to their boss when it comes to recognizing they are the problem. A direct report or peer will not be successful attempting to lead a *high-achieving performer* because they are not willing to devote the time developing meaningful relationships. Mainly because it required too much of their time, and generally they don't allocate time for relationship building. To be fair, I should point out that not all *high-achieving performers* fall into this category. But the only way to find out is to develop relationships with all managers so we can learn who falls into this category and who doesn't. It's simple really, we've gotten what we've rewarded because people do what they see. We've created this environment and the way we solve it begins with us. We have to agree today to either be part of the solution or part of the problem.

"I believe the solution begins with the Relational Leadership Model, which is a leadership model that Thomas, our leadership consultant, has shared with me." Taylar turns toward the whiteboard to draw the completed model Thomas finally shared with her last night during their meeting. When she's finished drawing the model, she turns back around to face the team to continue. "I would like for each of us to agree right now we will put this theory into practice in each of our divisions by meeting with each of our managers on a biweekly basis for a period of six months. At the end of six months, we will meet again and decide as a group how to proceed." Taylar makes eye contact with every member of the team to ensure their commitment to the plan, and each person nods their head in agreement or verbally says, "Yes," until she reaches David.

She thought they had made progress last week. Why is he still resisting this? Taylar feels as though she has no other choice but to call him out in front of his peers. "David, maybe I am wrong here, but it feels as though you are either disagreeing with the explanation I've just given or you do not want to go along with the rest of the team on this process. If I am wrong, I want you to tell me I am. You have my permission." Taylar calmly responds.

Everyone at the table stops what they're doing and looks directly at David to listen to his response. "Taylar, I've spent time with the people on my staff getting to know them by taking them to lunch, but still you're telling me I'm the problem."

> Taylar is very careful not to match David's level of emotion when responding.

Taylar is very careful not to match David's level of emotion when responding, so she begins with a question. "David, when was the last time you did some of the things you just mentioned?" Taylar persists.

David shakes his head in frustration, still not believing he's the source of the problem, hoping someone else on the team will speak up in his defense, like Bill. *Why isn't Bill taking up for me? We've been the dynamic duo for the past couple of years.* David turns his head to glance Bill's way when he realizes Bill is staring a hole right through him. He realizes in an instant that Bill will not bail him out, so he turns his head back to the front so he can respond to Taylar's question. "It's been a while, I guess."

"David, do you realize what motivates a person changes over their lifetime?" Before David has time to reply, Taylar continues explaining. "The reason we must develop relationships with all of our leaders and then continue working on them over time is because people experience death, cancer, child births, divorce, and many other things that affect their personal lives. And what affects their personal life will spill over into their work life, and this is where most leaders check out because this takes too much of their time to help work through these issues with an employee."

Finally David relents and agrees to move forward. "Taylar, I will agree to meet with every leader in my division for six months. Can we just get going and talk about this relational leadership thing?"

Taylar isn't sure if he's giving in to peer pressure or if he's really decided to buy into the change. Either way, they are moving forward for the time being. "As I was saying before, this is the Relational Leadership Model.

Example 7

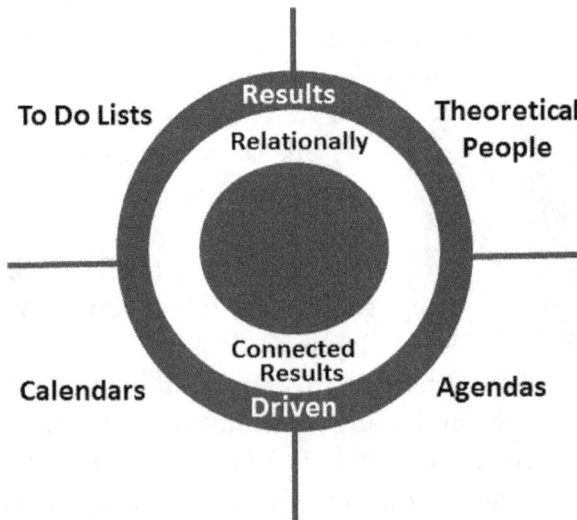

Results
Relationally

To Do Lists

Theoretical
People

Calendars

Connected
Results
Driven

Agendas

"This is the next step in the model, and I wanted to show you what it looked like before we begin by breaking it down step by step. Most people recognize this image as what you might see if you were looking through a scope on a rifle with a bull's eye in the center. The words in the four squares are the methods people use to obtain results and manage their time. Some people use to-do lists or task lists, some use calendars, some use agendas, and some use theoretical knowledge to drive results. Many people use two of these methods to drive results. For example, I use calendars and to-do lists to drive results. Would anyone of you disagree?" Taylar asks the group to consider her methods. "I would like each of you to take a few minutes and write down the methods you use to get results. When you're finished, we'll take a ten minute personal break and come back and share what each of you has chosen with the group."

The group walks back in from break talking about what they always talk about—sports, movies, exercising, and the latest books they've read. They take their seats ready to begin the next session. Taylar begins. "Would someone like to volunteer to go first? But before you say anything, this is how we'll learn what each person uses. I would like the rest of the team to guess what methods each person uses to get results so we can learn how well we know each other."

Jim volunteers to go first. "Who would like the first shot to guess Jim's method?" Taylar asks.

"I would," Jacob says. "I believe Jim uses calendars to manage his time and get results. He has a different color for each activity he plans to include using a different color for each of our divisions so anyone can see where he is at a glance."

Taylar waits for Jacob to finish before asking. "Would anyone like to add to what Jacob has said?" Everyone turns and looks at the other, and each one of them is shaking their head no, so Taylar asks Jim. "Is the team correct?"

"Yes, they are." Jim and Jacob do their traditional fist bump they do when they're together.

> Taylar recognizes the team is starting to lighten up and get into the activity.

Taylar recognizes the team is starting to lighten up and get into the activity so she asks, "Who would like to be next?"

Karen raises her hand and volunteers. "I'll go next."

Bill raises his hand to answer. "I would like to take a shot at this one if you don't mind."

Taylar answers, "Go right ahead."

"I think Karen uses task lists and calendars to manage her time and get results."

"Well, team, what do you think?"

Almost in unison, the team says, "We agree."

Without Taylar having to ask Karen, she lets the team know they are correct. "Perfect. Am I that easy to read?" Karen humorously asks.

The team erupts in laughter at that question—everyone except David. And he is sure he is about to witness some sort of group hug, and he can't stand it. He has to leave immediately. He needs to make up an excuse to get out of this. But reality sinks in when he hears Taylar say his name. "David, are you still with us?"

"Sadly, yes."

That comment causes the room to get eerily silent. Without hesitation, Jim decides to respond. "Come on, David, lighten up. This is kind of fun." The rest of the team joins in. "Yeah, David, just lighten up."

Taylar decides that David should be next. "Who would like to guess David's methods?"

"I will," Jim says. "I think David is a theoretical person."

Taylar asks the rest of the team. "Do you agree with Jim?"

"Yes." Nearly the entire team responds to this one.

"David, are they correct?" Taylar asks.

"No, I use my calendar and task lists to get results," David fires back.

"Okay, let's see if we can talk ourselves through this one. Do you spend time weekly planning all of your work?" Taylar asks.

"Well, I use my calendar to schedule some of my meetings."

"That's a great start, David, but let's figure out which meetings are the ones that normally receive your attention. Are your weekly staff meetings on your calendar?"

"Yes."

"Are your weekly production meetings on your calendar?"

"Yes."

"That's great. Those are both very important meetings and should be on everyone's calendars. Are your weekly safety, quality, environmental, and housekeeping meetings are your calendar?"

"No, they aren't."

"Are your one-on-ones or team huddles with your direct reports on your calendar?"

"No, they aren't."

"Well, we have some place to start then."

There is a knock on the door, and the administrative assistant steps in to inform Taylar it is noon and the food has been delivered. Taylar says, "We will resume after lunch. There will be a one-hour break, and everyone should return here by 1:00 p.m so we can start our team building activity and that will take the remainder of the day."

CHAPTER 21

Executive Staff Meeting Number Two

Taylar begins the meeting at precisely eight o'clock. "Who has something they can share about a relationship with a direct report? Remember not to share anything you've been told in confidence. We only want generalities or things we've been told that is okay to share with others. We must develop trusting relationships during this process."

Jacob raises his hand to be the first to share with the executive staff. "I have learned what each of my direct reports need for feedback, how they want to be rewarded, and what I need to do so they trust me and trust each other."

> We must develop trusting relationships during this process.

"That's fantastic, Jacob. Thank you for sharing. I know you've been working very hard to make a difference in your division over the past month, and we can all see by the latest financial statements that your division is starting to climb up out of the cellar. Your division has closed the gap on number three."

The team immediately starts clapping and congratulating Jacob on his division's accomplishments. This is the first time in a long time the executive staff has recognized Jacob on an accomplishment. This is also the one thing that energizes him the most. It's like charging a DC battery, filling his tank up, and Taylar knows it and that is one of the reasons why she brought it up at this point in the staff meeting.

Bill raises his hand to volunteer to go second. Taylar motions for him to go ahead. "I've started by asking each of my direct reports how I can increase the trust in our relationship with each of them. A few said very little at first. I suspect it is because we have never really had that type of conversation before, so they weren't really sure how to take me. But during the second meeting, they opened up a little more, and we started talking about hobbies and sports, which got them loosened up even more. I'm confident in a couple more meetings, we will be able to share much more.

PART 5

The Big Decision

CHAPTER 22

Something Has Got to Change

Taylar parks in the visitor's parking spaces as usual when she arrives at David's division. It's been three months since their first meeting, and he has made very little progress. She's growing very concerned he's not going to make it. Maybe he just isn't cut out to lead people, at least not this many. The meetings she's had with some of his direct reports and several of his frontline leaders indicate nothing has really changed at his division. He's still the autocratic micromanager he has always been. He appears to still be living in a state of crisis. He can't seem to accomplish anything by planning ahead. She's not sure how his employees are hanging on.

> Maybe he just isn't cut out to lead people.

Taylar climbs the stairs to the front office and walks through the sliding door. Like always, she's greeted as soon she walks into the lobby. Everyone exchanges pleasantries and small talk, mentioning things like the weather, whether or not Taylar experienced any travel issues, and what the next big plans are for RMT Technologies. Taylar excuses herself and walks into the hallway to David's office.

When she reaches his office, she can hear him talking on the phone, so she waits to knock until he's wrapped up the conversation. Just as he's about to place the receiver on the hook, she knocks on the door.

David stands up to greet her, and they both walk toward the conference table and sit down. Taylar initiates the conversation by asking the now standard questions. "David, since the last time we've met, have I done anything that has made you mad or frustrated?"

"No, you haven't."

"Since the last time we met, have I failed to meet a commitment I've made?"

"No, you haven't."

"How are your meetings going with your direct reports?"

"Slow. It still seems like they aren't really motivated and don't like the changes you're making."

"I'm making," Taylar says sternly. "I didn't realize I was making that many changes here at your division." Taylar's demeanor has turned serious. "David, after talking with your peers, your direct reports, and some of your frontline leaders, it seems your behavior hasn't really changed. Are you even trying to make an honest attempt to change?" Taylar asks.

"Taylar, I think if you would just let me lead this division the way they need to be led, you'd see I'm right. I don't trust them to make decisions. Not good ones anyway. They never get projects right or completed on time unless I'm out there constantly pushing them. They're just lazy."

> David, it sounds to me as though your employees do not trust you.

"David, it sounds to me as though your employees do not trust you."

"Trust me!" David exclaims loudly.

"David, you are confusing laziness and lack of effort with a lack of trust. All of the signs point toward a low-trust relationship with them. You have no speed in your organization because your team doesn't trust you. If you had trust, you could push them harder because then they would know you were pushing for the right reasons, which is to make the team better."

"Taylar, we've been the second best performing division for two years. Why do we need to change anything?"

"Any chance you would like to be number one? Taylar quickly responds.

David isn't going to change, and no amount of talking and coaching from her will make it happen. At this point, Taylar knows what she has to do. He can probably see what's coming next.

"David, this isn't really working out any longer. We seem to be going in two different directions. We are trying to change our organization to have a more servant leadership style, and you seem to be stuck in an autocratic, dictator-style leadership mode. We are not micromanagers. If we have to micromanage, then we've hired the wrong person. We are working to empower our people and then unleash them to reach their full potential."

David appears to be getting more upset the longer Taylar talks. "Taylar, why are you doing this to me?" David says it like he is totally surprised, actually more like offended by the fact Taylar has asked these questions.

"David, your peers don't respect you. Your direct reports don't respect you. Most of your division doesn't respect you or trust you. I don't see another way around this decision any longer. I would like to offer you a six-month severance for your resignation as the general manager of this division. We are headed in two different directions, and I think you will be happier if you were working somewhere else."

"Taylar, I'm the only person who can run this division. No one else has what it takes."

"We'll find the right person, and your team will be just fine." Taylar pulls out a document from her backpack sets it down on the table. Taylar slides it across the table to David. "This is a severance offer to continue paying your salary and insurance for six months in exchange for your resignation."

"I'm not staying anywhere I'm not wanted, but let me tell you, I'm not the problem here. Give me about an hour, and I'll have my stuff boxed up and be out of here."

"That'll work."

"Where do I sign?" David grudgingly asks.

"You need to sign on the blank line at the bottom."

David pulls out a pen and signs the document and then slides it back across the table to Taylar. Taylar looks it over and says, "Okay, its official."

David stands up and walks to his desk and picks up the phone. "I need someone to bring me three or four medium-sized boxes to my office."

Taylar stands up, walks into the hallway, and immediately calls Karen. "It's done. He signed the document. I need you to remove all his access from our network."

"Will do."

"Thanks, Karen. I'll talk with you later."

When Taylar finishes her phone call, the boxes arrive. David immediately starts throwing stuff in the boxes as fast as he can. David was right; in forty minutes, all his stuff are packed in three boxes, and he is walking to the parking lot.

Thirty minutes after David is gone, the staff is assembled in the conference room. Taylar takes a deep breath and then walks in. As she scans the faces in the room, she can see the look of fear and unknown written on all of their faces. Taylar exhales. "Let me begin by saying no one in this room is in trouble so you all can breathe now. The second thing is David no long works here because he has resigned. I want—" Taylar is immediately interrupted by the cheering and applauding that has spontaneously erupted from the staff. She's completely taken off guard because she thought they might be happy but not like this.

PART 6

Moving On

CHAPTER 23

Executive Staff Meeting
Number Three

In two short days following the meeting with David, the executive staff is set to have their third meeting. Everyone shows up a few minutes early, as usual, grabs some coffee, juice, and fruit, and then starts the normal small talk on sports, movies, their most recent workout schedules, current events, the looming political race, and the latest books they're reading. Taylar walks into the board room at precisely five minutes until eight o'clock, ready to begin. The rest of the staff begins taking their unassigned but regular seats because each of them are creatures of habit, whether they will admit it or not. Taylar begins exactly on time and is prepared to stray from the agenda to discuss what has transpired over the past couple of days. She clears her throat and starts the explanation.

"After a considerable amount of thought and reflection, I've reached a decision with a clear conscious. The decision was made for David and RMT Technologies to part ways. While I was meeting with him two days ago, we mutually reached the decision and decided it would be best for both him and us if we moved forward without him. He will continue to be our friend, if he wants to, but he just won't be part of our team. Who would like to ask a question about this?"

Bill motioned that he would like to say something. "Who will be replacing David at his division?"

"I'm glad you asked. I was thinking Caleb would be a good choice, but I wanted to discuss the list of potential candidates with our team to determine who you think is ready to make this transition," Taylar explains.

> As Taylar scans the group no one appears to be surprised or disappointed with the decision.

As Taylar scans the group, she notices no one appears to be surprised or disappointed with the decision—a good confirmation that she's made the right decision. Now it's time to move forward.

PART 7

The Overview

Getting Great Results

I have been blessed by God with a few natural abilities and talents, and if it weren't for Him, I would be nothing or have nothing. All I am is because of Him. My wife, daughter, parents, grandparents, sister, and brother have also been very positive influences in my life and have helped guide me during the good and the bad. They have never failed to be there even when I messed up, and believe me, I have—just ask my brother and sister. Well, on second thought, don't.

> I've been influenced by many world people during my professional career, which has helped me develop into the person and leader I am today.

I've been influenced by many worldly people during my professional career, which has helped me develop into the person and leader I am today. During this process, I've learned the good and the bad from these people, concentrating on using the good ideas and concepts I learned to help develop teams and people. The one person who has influenced me the most during my leadership journey is Dr. John C. Maxwell, which is a little ironic because I never met the man until after this book was written. I have read nearly all his books and listened to about one hundred of his audio lessons dating back to 2005.

You can also see influences in my behavior, language, and writing from the following people—Abraham Maslow, Stephen

Covey, Stephen M.R. Covey, Jon Gordon, Patrick Lencioni, Robert Greenleaf, Dr. Henry Cloud, Ken Blanchard, Mark Miller, Andy Stanley, Earl Nightingale, Frederick Herzberg, Marcus Buckingham, Donald Clifton, Stephen Ambrose, John Grisham, Tom Pace, Stuart Keeton, Jason Langley, Vernon Butts, Wayne McCoy, Wayne Muirheid, Randy Watson, Tony Rankins, Joseph Simonelli, my wife Mary, and I'm sure many others.

I wanted to include this summary to make it easier for some to use and apply the concepts of the Relational Leadership Model. No one ever gets better without making a conscious decision to do so, and leadership always begins with self. Today you can make the decision to be better. Here's how.

Example 8

- The model was designed as a hierarchy with *Great Results* in the center of the bull's eye. This level cannot be achieved without developing high-trust relationships. People will always perform at a higher level when they are led instead of being managed. I could continue to explain it further for many pages but would recommend you read *The Speed of Trust* by Stephen M.R. Covey because he does a good job.[4]

- The ring surrounding Great Results is *Relationally Connected Results*. It's based on developing and equipping people and teams through relationships in order to achieve results. This cannot happen without having a passion for wanting to help develop people. And you cannot develop and equip people unless you sit down and talk with them on a regular basis. This isn't the same as a simple hello when walking by their cubicle. Remember, your people need your time and attention most. You must be committed to learning about their family, habits, hobbies, personality quirks, and their passion. This is known as the holistic approach to leadership, and yes, it takes time, but it's worth it.

Here are some of the questions I've developed over the years that I ask during one-on-ones to help develop my relationship with a direct report, peer, or supervisor. When starting a new relationship, I always ask each person to provide three responses to these questions to help establish a baseline. Then you must periodically follow up to gain momentum in building the relationship and to confirm their answers.

1. *How do you like to be rewarded?* This is to determine if the person is internally or externally motivated. By the way, *all* people need encouragement, not just externally motivated ones.
2. *How do you like to be given feedback?* Most people prefer the praise in public and criticize in private philosophy, and you should follow that viewpoint if you want to lead successfully. Feedback should be given monthly during the one-on-one and should be used as a coaching tool to help people perform at a higher level. Waiting to give feedback until an annual performance review should *never* happen. Everything an employee is told during the performance review should be just that—a review of previous conversations. Also remember that feedback should be a two-

way street, meaning you need to allow your direct reports, peers, and supervisor to provide you with feedback.

3. *How do I earn your trust?* Trust is always earned and never given. Trust is earned over time little by little. Every time you keep a commitment, spend time developing the relationship, add value to them, and keep your word, you make a deposit that increases trust.

As the relationship begins to develop, I have a different set of questions I ask. I've learned the hard way; if you don't ask the right question, you don't always hear what someone really wants to say. I've had people act quite relieved by giving them an opening by asking these questions.

1. *Since the last time we met, what I have done that has made you mad or frustrated?* Sometimes people won't be forthcoming with information so you have to almost pry it out of them.

2. *Since the last time we met have I failed to meet a commitment I've made to you?* I have a pretty good memory and have been blessed with that strength, but on rare occasions, even I forget something. So it's very important to ask this question to allow the relationship to develop high trust. And remember if someone shares something with you here, you need to ask for forgiveness and then figure out how to meet the commitment you made.

3. *If you could do anything, what would it be?* I have two questions I use to get this answer. I'm trying to learn what really energizes them. Every leader needs to make sure every person is working in the right job. Here is the other way I ask this question.

4. *What are you passionate about?* This question is designed to correct potential performance problems. The key is if you are going to be candid with a person and provide constructive criticism, you must be willing to accept the same in

return. Otherwise, your leadership looks like the model do as I say, not as I do.

5. *What is the greatest lesson you've learned that you could share with someone?* This question helps you understand what they've experienced and potentially avoid any major mistakes they have made.

6. *What was your biggest failure, and what did you learn from it?* This will help you determine if failure has caused them to stop growing and learning. Attitude plays a huge part in failure because everyone fails and makes mistakes, it's what we learn from them that sets us apart from everyone else.

7. *I have something we need to talk about. It's possible I might have gotten this wrong, and if I have, I give you permission to tell me I am wrong, but here's the behavior I've noticed.* This is where you would insert the behavior, action, language, or etc. that needs to be addressed. But remember, they need to be given the opportunity to push back if they feel you've gotten it wrong. Listening to understand is very important here.

   - The ring surrounding relationally connected results is *Results Driven.* This is the level where someone gets promoted to a leadership position and must learn the basics about leading people. If they try to lead people from this level too long, they create an environment of low trust, low morale, and high turnover. The buzzword these days seems to be *low engagement*, so I better use it too. This is also the area where I've seen a number of people try and fail over and over again because they don't understand people or how to lead. I call these people *High-Performing Achievers.*

They normally start off well producing results, and their boss thinks they are doing a good job. But it takes time to recognize how these *High-Performing Achievers* are leading. The most common leadership style they use is autocratic. Sometimes they throw in a little intimidation just for general purpose. Many of them love to micromanage, and some yell at their employees in front of their peers. Some of them live in a constant state of crisis. People with this behavior type believe they cannot function well unless their teams are working in crisis mode, which creates cyclical results. As long as they are out pushing their team by micromanaging them, they deliver results. But as soon as the leader turns around and heads for the office, the effort is reduced.

I typically see this behavior in organizations that lack leadership training to help these new leaders develop. If a person doesn't receive the tools necessary to develop themselves, they do what got them promoted. In the end, these organizations get the results they reward.

Each of the behaviors in the Relational Leadership Model represent a method people use to get results. Three of the four are usually easy to relate with while the fourth, theoretical people, is a little abstract. I am sure there are other behaviors you've seen and could insert into the model like personality assessment types, but these are the four I choose. *Calendars* are one of the methods I use to manage my time and get results partly because I am a relationship-based person. I learned this behavior from *The 7 Habits of Highly Effective People* by Stephen R. Covey.[5] I spend time weekly planning the things that are the most important to me in both my professional and personal life. *To-Do Lists* is another one of the methods I use to manage my time weekly and get results. This is a conventional method for many people who are task-based, and several books have been written about the importance of using lists.

Agendas are another method people use to drive results and manage time. You can see both task-based and relationship-based people using this style frequently. The other half of this method is describing political people. The agenda they have is to get promoted, get a better title, or simply use people to get to the top. I can't stand this behavior type, and when you find these people in your organization, you need to promote them to a former employee.

Theoretical People is the last of the four methods. I struggled to settle on what method to use for some time in the last square, but I've encountered this behavior more often than I care to admit. One half of these people are highly intelligent and fit into the category of being book smart but lacking common sense. These people struggle to communicate. They are a little eccentric and lack some social skills. Employees don't readily respond well to this leader type because they have a hard time connecting with them.

The ones in this half of the method are highly task-based and solve problems using math and science. They can have issues with seeing everything black and white, very little gray. These leaders can be effective but have to be careful to not micromanage their employees. They seek perfection.

Leadership is never easy, and it takes continuous effort. If you want to continue developing, you must be committed to continually learning. Your team depends on you to continue developing into a better leader so you can continue developing them.

NOTES

1   John C. Maxwell, *The 360 Degree Leader: Developing Your Influence fron Anywhere in the Organization* (Nashville: Thomas Nelson, 2005), pg. 263.
2   Ibid.
3   Suzanne Massie, "The Reagan Years 1984–1988," 23 March 2014, http://www. suzannemassie.com/reaganYears.html, Accessed on March 23, 2014.
4   Stephen M.R. Covey, *The Speed of Trust: The One Thing That Changes Everything* (Free Press, 2006).
5   Stephen R. Covey, *The 7 Habits of Highly Effective People* (Franklin Covey, 1998).

ABOUT THE AUTHOR

Robert Epperly is the director of Webco University for Webco Industries. He is first a child of God and second a thought leader and equipper of people. Robert is a leadership expert that has trained and coached hundreds of people to higher performance for more than a decade. Robert and his wife, Mary, reside in Sand Springs, Oklahoma. You can find Robert on LinkedIn (Robert Epperly, MBA), Twitter (@leadself), and on Facebook.

CPSIA information can be obtained
at www.ICGtesting.com
Printed in the USA
BVHW031343200521
607790BV00006B/766

9 781636 300009